MW00744294

California Out of the Box
An Interdisciplinary History Curriculum

Prehistory to 1930s

Grades 3-6

By Christine Echeverri

CARRIER SHELL CURRICULUM
www.carriershellcurriculum.com

© 2018 Christine Echeverri
All Rights Reserved.
No part of this work may be reproduced or transmitted in any form or by any
means, electronic or mechanical, including photocopying and recording, or by
any information storage or retrieval system without prior written permission of
the copyright owner unless such copying is expressly permitted by USA copyright
law, or unless it complies with the Photocopying and Distribution Policy on page
xvii.

Address requests for permissions to make copies to:
info@carriershellcurriculum.com.
Please include a phone number or e-mail address when contacting us.

Printed in the USA
ISBN: 978-172-66722-76
Version 1.2
Code: CA104

For updates and corrections see "Errata" on our website.

To find out more information about Carrier Shell Curriculum
and other lesson plans and resources, go to
www.carriershellcurriculum.com.

Cover Design Front cover: illustration by Camille Echeverri. Back cover: *The
Unique Map of California* is used with permission from David Rumsey Map Collection, www.davidrumsey.com.

Illustrations Tables, figures, photographs, and keys are either drawn and designed
by Christine Echeverri or from public domain sources, except where noted next to
image.

Typeset using LaTeX

Contents

III ¡*Oro!*
The Great Rush for Gold   92

6 Unit Introduction   93

7 *By the Great Horn Spoon!*   94

IV ¡Terremoto!
California Jolted: The San Francisco Earthquake   146

List of Tables

List of Figures

Organic Learning: Developing Our Kids' Carrier Shells

The Morro Bay Shell Shop is the subject of many fond memories going back to my childhood. On one of my excursions there as an adult, a particular shell caught my eye: An ordinary mollusk shell...with shells from other creatures glued to the top. Why had someone gone to the trouble of doing that, and why was such an outlandish craft piece being sold in this shell shop? The clerk was kind enough to educate me: the artist had been the animal itself, moving around the seabed, collecting other shells and fragments of debris and cementing them to itself. I was intrigued. I had to learn more.

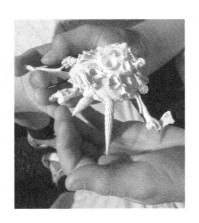

This animal is a mollusk from the class *gastropoda*, which in Greek means "stomach-foot." Gastropods include snails and slugs found on both land and sea; limpets, conches, sea slugs, and abalones fall into this class. The carrier snail makes its shell as many other gastropods do; it grows and radiates in a spiral shape from the center of the shell. This particular animal includes one unique feature. As it moves along on the ocean floor it finds other rocks and shells lying around; now and then with its foot, it lifts one up and holds it against its exterior, secreting a calcium carbonate glue to cement it in place. Moreover, ocean organisms can fall on the animal; even sponges three times as big as the shell can be found added in this way. This gastropod ends up having a shell that is eclectic, strange, and beautiful.

Growing up, while attending public school, I was fortunate to have a mom who went to great lengths to immerse my sister and me in a rich variety of experiences. Camping...hiking...helping at homeless shelters...sailing on whale watching trips: these experiences were committed to our beings as emotional memories, not just detached facts in our brains. Like shell fragments added to the carrier snail, we allowed these memories to stick and become a part of who we are.

Whether in conventional school or homeschool, families and teachers have a great opportunity to help their students in creating their own beautiful carrier shells. With thoughtful choices about study topics and timing, parents and educators can help their students organically formulate a frame that reflects the values and the landscape of that child's family traditions. When the student participates in choosing which shells to add, his or her shell will be recognizable as a shell crafted from that family, including pieces special to the student. Parents and teachers know the individuality of their students. Through our unique approach to learning, this curriculum will assist in the addition of educational gems to add to a young child's education. Like shell building, it will be organic, self-determined, and unique.

California Curriculum

It is in the spirit of the creativity of a carrier shell that this curriculum is written.

The educational aim is to provide a bearing for students – both in schools and homeschool settings – to consider the story of California. As the carrier shell adds other shells to its own, I have chosen historical fiction as a base to anchor facets of the story of California – its major habitats, history, ethnic make-up, geography, and science. While the five stories are not historically factual, they do provide a student-appropriate, well-researched context with which these other topics can be explored, in ways that the story will be anchored and truly become a part of that "eclectic" shell. I have chosen to go as far as the 1930s, as ending the story here gives a good flow and reasonable workload in the story of pre-modern California. Certainly California has developed much since then, with an ever increasing population and demand for diminishing resources such as water; these developments could very well be the subject of future curriculum studies. Supplemental resources are listed in the Future Study Resources section. Additionally, although books such as the *Island of the Blue Dolphins* are not usually introduced to a third grader, in a homeschool/progressive school environment, this book can be utilized as a read-aloud. (I know young kids can benefit from hearing quality stories that might be above their reading "level." My husband's father read *Uncle Tom's Cabin* to him at age 5, and he has good memories of it!)

In the school environment, it is important for educators to know this curriculum is based on California State Standards for 4th grade history through the 1930s (State Board of Education, History-Social Science Framework 2016). Additionally, schools that emphasize visual learning will enjoy using visual references such as Google Earth, Youtube videos, and ongoing space and encouragement in the curriculum for students to draw their responses. This curriculum, however, does not teach visual arts methods.

Another goal is to help children become reflective about their young lives. Often we think of children "doing" and adults "thinking." However, if educators can introduce the idea that children can reflect, and reflect deeply, and channel those deep thoughts into creative responses such as poetry, art, and making collections, we might have more adults who are living peaceful lives and not running away from challenges. Why not add the shells of reflection to the base shell also?

The final goal of this curriculum is to introduce science, not through discrete, disembodied facts (i.e., – memorizing structures of biology, animal, and plant kingdoms), but through affirming what students observe and hear, through the context of story. Curiosity begins with perception, and curiosity can be a powerful motivator. There are surely fewer reasons better than the desire to satisfy one's curiosity for investing time and effort to develop deep understanding of a thing. Thus, I have emphasized *observation* and *personal experience* in this curriculum, as opposed to the "facts-based" (read: "memorization") approach familiar to most parents from their own elementary schooling. Like the carrier shell, science becomes something added to the shell, and attached to the shell, because it becomes owned by the shell in the animal's decision to cement that shell on. I aim for personal ownership in explaining the world of science.

If, as you are going through this curriculum, some of the areas of exploration are not intuitive or simply won't work for your family or educational environment, don't sweat it. Glued on, that shell was not meant to be.

With these goals in mind, I invite you to explore the land that we call California.

How to Use This Curriculum

Overview

This curriculum contains five units, the first two units are linked – part 1 and 2 (one chapter book each), and the subsequent three units including one chapter book each. Interspersed between these books are selected stories involving children's adventures in natural environments in California, readings from the *National Audubon Society Field Guide to California*, excerpts from Mark Twain, and other research and reflections, that are largely web based. The library would also work for research – but the idea is to briefly look into things. This curriculum is dense in its breadth.

This curriculum is designed for a 36-week time frame, with each of the five parts taking approximately seven weeks.

In a traditional classroom, California history is taught in the 4th grade. However, in the homeschooling/progressive school environment, teachers may choose to study disciplines in grade years different from traditional schools. This curriculum has been adapted so it may be used for students in grades 3-6. Beyond history, this interdisciplinary curriculum covers literature, science (life science, earth science, and social science), religious traditions, anthropology, art, and storytelling.

Additionally, homeschool families should see Suggestions for Younger Siblings for age-appropriate resources that will allow younger family members to follow along with important aspects of the story.

Key Concepts

The words that you find written in **bold** highlight various concepts which are woven throughout the story. While more complicated vocabulary could have been chosen to describe certain anthropological and scientific concepts, I have decided to err on the side of having an intuitive curriculum, one that works for ages 8-12. Complex words do not embody the reality they seek to describe, and they are often loaded with assumptions and baggage. The emphasis is on story and providing a holistic view, rather than on acute rigor.

Important: Encouraging Student Engagement

Big Questions In most sections you will find a question to challenge abstract thinking before getting into a more detailed discussion. You may read these questions before the literature selection or after. These questions roughly correlate to the themes in the chapter, but the true purpose is both to help frame the learning experience and to encourage students to dig deep to explain why something is so. If these questions stimulate good conversations, stick with them; do not worry about getting to the comprehension questions.

Comprehension, Review, Bonus, and Reflection Questions Sometimes if young children are asked to summarize a story they have read or movie they have seen, they will verbalize what they believe the adult wants to hear. Their own reflections and what they have actually learned can be emotionally much deeper. For that reason, don't feel that you must grill your students. Allow your students to have their own feelings and memories of the material.

Each of the 5 units will have its own driving questions. This approach is different from using questions to prompt kids to recite major events or plot twists in each chapter. The well-developed characters in these books have real things to reveal about their lives, ethnicity, and experiences in California.

Personally, when I homeschooled, my children did not want to speak or converse about their reflections on stories. I knew they were listening, though! Therefore, chapter comprehension questions can be discussed, written, sketched, or even omitted at your discretion.

Oral Narration Option   In lieu of the questions, you may also choose to have your students give you an oral narration or summary of what they remember from the day's reading. If they draw a blank, help them get their juices flowing by asking them to tell you about the events or characters in the story. They should put their thoughts in a few complete sentences. At the 3rd grade level or below, you may choose to have them say the narration, and then (you, the teacher) write it on a white board as they say it, and they can recopy the dictation in their Composition Book. A good rule of thumb is one sentence for each grade, so that the 6th grader would write 6 sentences. Really important to this option is that you as the teacher must be prepared that the events or parts of the story that your students remember may not be the ones that you think are important. So, it is vital that you allow them to say the aspects that *they* view are important. No answers are provided for narration, as this will vary student by student.

Answer Keys

Both sample answers to comprehension questions (written in *italics*) and mapwork keys are located in the sections where they are taught. However, there are a few items such as: How We Came Tracker, Habitat Tracker A, Habitat Tracker B, California Map, and a few other keys that can be found in the Key section in the Appendix, as these resources run throughout two or more sections and will be easier to locate at the end.

End of Unit Questions (5th and 6th Grade)

At the end of each unit there are questions that can be used either for a conversation, writing, or further projects. These questions give older students a chance to reflect and draw connections between different time periods and disciplines.

Should You Need to Trim the Curriculum

If you find the pacing is too brisk, here are some sections that can be omitted or moved around and still retain the backbone of California curriculum:

1. Unit I

   - Mythology: The Earth Dragon, page 27
   - Poetry Reflection: Time, page 38
   - History: Santa Catalina Island, page 42
   - Science: Plant Observation & Collection, page 21 (may be moved to Week 13 or 14 to give more time earlier)

2. Unit II

   - Either choose Religion: Our Lady of Guadalupe, page 70 or Religious Traditions: *Las Posadas*, page 71

3. Unit III

   - Geography: Treasure Maps, page 96
   - Unique Habitat: The Galápagos Islands, page 100
   - History: CD Parkhurst, page 104

4. Unit IV

   - Mark Twain and the "Great" Earthquake in San Francisco, page 152
   - Historical Places: Chinatown, SF, page 161 (may be moved to Week 26, 27, or 28)
   - A Closer Look: Using Figurative Language, page 164
   - Geological Research: California's Major Quakes, page 179
   - Research: Internet vs. Books, page 186

5. Unit V

- U.S. Citizenship: How to Apply, page 225 (introduce site, but omit exercise if running short on time)

Foreword

One of my earliest memories I have of my grandma was driving to land which was being developed in Thousand Oaks, California. The developers were turning over the dirt to prepare the land for the homes which were going to be built. My mom, my grandma, and I were there to see if there were any Native American arrowheads or grinding bowls that may have been turned over in the dirt.

When I went to my grandma's house, she would show me her dresser drawers which were not filled with clothing – but with hundreds of rocks! She was an amazing collector: old California roses, flowering succulents, beads, and minerals. My mother was equally in love with this world – we took trip after trip to many areas in California, the Southwest, the East Coast, the Chicago area, and even Europe to explore science, art, and history.

My time in K-12 formal education was spent on developing visual arts skills. For my undergraduate education, I entered UCLA as an art major. Realizing I already knew a lot about art, I became restless and decided to explore art history and anthropology of the non-Western world. I loved my study so much, I added comparative religion to my program. I then worked as an art teacher at a group home, and later ran my own floral design business.

After my undergraduate degree, I went to Asia; I learned I loved economics – maybe through all of the bargaining I did! I came right back and I completed a MA in economics. Additionally, somewhere in there, I had 3 kids.

My own children were in school when I realized there was learning that my husband and I considered important, that was not getting through to them in that setting. Because I was fortunate to not have to work outside the home, when my daughter was in 4th grade, we began our homeschooling adventure, which continued for 3 years. I loved being in "school" with my kids. I learned and re-learned much in those 3 years.

During our experiences, my desire grew to develop what we were learning for educators and homeschool families. I had been spending a lot of time developing my own curriculum because, when we got to California history, I couldn't find the exact resource I was looking for. This frustration led me to move my kids back to a school environment so that I could develop my approach.

This curriculum is my foray into synthesizing seemingly divergent topics. My hope is that this curriculum presents these different areas to give students a broad, yet interesting springboard for exploring the world.

Christine Echeverri, MA
June 2018

Book List

For other supplies, see list at the beginning of each unit.

1. Listed in the order used

   - Stories Combo Set: *The California Coast* reader and *California Out of the Box Supplement*, available at carriershellcurriculum.com

     [The Stories Combo Set replaces the out of print *Stories from Where We Live: The California Coast* (Sara St. Antoine, ISBN 1-57131-631-0) and paperback edition *The California Coast: A Literary Field Guide (Stories from Where We Live)*, (ISBN 1-57131-653-1).]

   - *National Audubon Society Field Guide to California* (used in all units - ISBN 978-0-679-44678-1)

   - *Island of the Blue Dolphins* (Scott O'Dell, ISBN 9780547-32861-4)

   - *Valley of the Moon: The Diary of María Rosalia de Milagros* (Sherry Garland, ISBN 0-439-08820-8)

   - *By the Great Horn Spoon!* (Sid Fleischman, ISBN 978031628612-1)

   - *The Earth Dragon Awakes* (Laurence Yep, ISBN 9780060008468)

   - *Esperanza Rising* (Pam Muñoz Ryan, ISBN 978-0-439-12042-5)

2. Recommended resources

   - *Death Trap: The Story of the La Brea Tar Pits* (Sharon Elaine Thompson, ISBN 0-8225-2851-7)

   - *A Gift For Abuelita* (Nancy Luenn, ISBN 0-87358-688-3)

- *Pedro: The Angel of Olvera Street* (Leo Politi, ISBN 978-0-89236-990-4)

- *Institute for Excellence in Writing (IEW) Student Resource Notebook* (contains the List of Banned [common] Words, with great word choice alternatives, ISBN 978-1-62341042-1)

Building Student Folder

Before beginning this curriculum, you will need to build the Student Folder. Purchase a 3-hole pocket folder and photocopy all blank master handouts that can be found in Appendices A and B. One copy of each page will suffice, with one exception. **Make 8 copies of the Habitat Description Sheets, table A.5**. Use a 3-hole punch on all sheets, and place in folder in the order they appear.

Photocopying and Distribution Policy:

The content, tables, original figures, and lists contained in this curriculum are copyrighted material owned by Carrier Shell Curriculum. Please do not reproduce reading lists, etc. on email lists or websites.

Families that purchase this curriculum may make photocopies of the tables and figures for use *within their family only*. Photocopying Student Folder pages so they can be resold is a violation of copyright.

Schools and co-ops may not photocopy any portion of the California Out of the Box curriculum. However, they may purchase an additional license ($100 per year), which allows for duplication by the school or co-op. For more information, please contact Carrier Shell Curriculum at info@carriershellcurriculum.com.

Activities Categorized by Type

Activities with asterisks appear in two or more categories.

Life Science

- Discovery, section 1.2.1, page 4.

- Habitat Study: Coast and Islands, section 2.2.2, page 18.

- Science: Plant Observation & Collection, section 2.2.4, page 21.

- Sea Otter Research: Chapters 23-24, section 2.4.2, page 29.

- Habitat Study: Chaparral, Coastal Scrub, and Oak Woodlands, section 3.1.3, page 46.

- State Symbol: The Grizzly Bear, section 5.4.6, page 79.

- Science: Water Potatoes? section 7.2.2, page 97.

- Unique Habitat: The Galápagos Islands, section 7.2.4, page 100.

- Habitat Study: Sierra Nevadas, section 7.4.1, page 107.

- Habitat Study: Coniferous Forests, section 7.5.2, page 115.

- Habitat Study: Marsh & Wetlands, section 9.4.3, page 181.

- Biology: The Monarch, section 10.2.3, page 197.

- Introduction to Unit V Projects*, section 10.2.4, page 199.

- Habitat Study: Deserts, section 11.2.3, page 216.

- Habitat Study: Grasslands of the Central Valley, section 11.3.3, page 220.

- Cutting Potato Eyes: *Las Papas*, pages 158-178, section 11.3.4, page 222.

Geography

- Looking at the Land: Map Introduction, section 1.2.3, page 9.

- The Americas: Chapters 1-2, section 7.1.1, page 94.

- Geography: Treasure Maps*, section 7.1.3, page 96.

- The Straits: Chapters 5-6, section 7.2.1, page 96.

- Land Exploration: State and National Parks, 7.6.2, page 119.

- Introduction to Unit V Projects*, section 10.2.4, page 199.

- Journey Mapping: How We Came*, section 11.2.5, page 218.

Social Studies

- Adaptations & Consequences: Chapters 8-9, section 2.2.1, page 16.

- Social Studies: Ethnicity, section 5.2.2, page 63.

- Going Deeper into Family Traditions: *Día de los Muertos*, section 5.2.5, page 66.

- Symbolism & Remembering Our Loved Ones*, section 5.2.6, page 67.

- *Californios* Introduced: Pages 39-59, section 5.3.1, page 69.

- Religion: Our Lady of Guadalupe*, section 5.3.2, page 70.

- Religious Traditions: *Las Posadas*, section 5.3.3, page 71.

- *Candlemas* and Groundhog Day: Pages 60-80, section 5.3.4, page 72.

- More on *Californios*: Pages 81-110, section 5.4.2, page 74.

- Drawing Comparisons: Venn Diagrams, section 5.4.3, page 75.

Poetry & Literature

Folklore & Mythology

Arts

Earth Science

History

Research

- Historical Research: Overview, section 2.5.4, page 35.

- Research: Using the *Audubon* Guide, section 5.1.1, page 53.

- Primary Sources: Gold Rush Stories*, section 7.7.1, page 124.

- Technology: Speedy Delivery of News and People*, section 7.8.1, page 131.

- Geological Research: California's Major Quakes*, section 9.4.2, page 179.

- Natural Resource: Water*, section 9.4.4, page 183.

- Research: Internet vs. Books, section 9.5.1, page 186.

- Newspaper Research: Review: The Story of California, section 10.2.1, page 193.

- Research: Oral History*, section 11.5.3, page 230.

Prehistory

- Pygmy Mammoths, section 3.0.2, page 39.

- Linking Time: Hollywood and the Pits, section 3.1.2, page 43.

- Geologic Time: Going from Mammoths Further Back to Dinosaurs, section 3.1.4, page 49.

Future Study Resources

- State Capitol Student Packet: geared for a student visit to the capitol in Sacramento, it goes over state symbols and branches of government. The packet serves as a nice review of the curriculum.

  https://capitolmuseum.ca.gov/images/
  capitolschoolpacket-studentversion.pdf

- California Museum: museum in Sacramento with downloadable activity sheets for teachers and parents, as well as hands-on projects.

  http://www.californiamuseum.org/

- Oakland Museum of California: this site features historical photos and interesting curriculum lessons (under Education and Resources for Teachers).

  http://museumca.org/

- *California History for Kids: Missions, Miners, and Moviemakers in the Golden State* by Katy S. Duffield. Concise resource that gives a broad look at important people and events, with historical pictures and activities.

- *California Plants and Animals* by Stephen Feinstein

- *City of Angels: In and Around Los Angeles* by Julie Jaskol & Brian Lewis

- *Gold Fever: California's Gold Rush* by Oakland Museum of California. This book has pictures of relics from the gold rush.

- *Gold Rush and Riches* by Paul Robert Walker

Suggestions for Younger Siblings

The following picture books, readily available from most libraries, will deepen the experience for students in early grade school.

1. California History Overview - can be read at any time

   - *Our California* by Pam Muñoz Ryan
   - *California, the Magic Island* by Doug Hansen

2. Unit I - for *Island of the Blue Dolphins*

   - *Ishi's Tale of Lizard* by Leanne Hinton and Susan L. Roth
   - *Two Bear Cubs: A Miwok Legend from California's Yosemite Valley* by Robert D. San Souci

3. Unit II - for *Valley of the Moon*

   - *Song of the Swallows* by Leo Politi
   - *A Gift For Abuelita* by Nancy Luenn (already recommended part of curriculum)
   - *Pedro: The Angel of Olvera Street* by Leo Politi (already a recommended part of curriculum)

4. Unit III - for *By the Great Horn Spoon!*

   - *The Camping Trip That Changed America* by Barb Rosenstock
   - *Gold Fever! Tales from the California Gold Rush* by Rosalyn Schanzer

- *Gold! Gold from the American River!* by Don Brown
- *Locomotive* by Brian Floca
- *Coolies* by Yin
- *The Transcontinental Railroad* by James P. Burger (historical overview)
- *This Is America, Charlie Brown* (DVD, Disc 2, Transcontinental Railroad episode)

5. Unit IV - for *The Earth Dragon Awakes*

- *Francis the Earthquake Dog* by Judith Ross Enderle & Stephanie Gordon Tessler
- *Angel Island* by Lori Mortenson
- *Julie the Rockhound* by Gail Langer Karwoski

6. Unit V - for *Esperanza Rising*

- *Calling the Doves/El Canto de las Palomas* by Juan Felipe Herrera
- *Dust for Dinner* by Ann Turner
- *A Picture Book of Cesar Chavez* by David A. Adler

Unit I

Antiguo

(Ancient, Former)

Part 1: Manzanita and Mammoths

Chapter 1

Unit Introduction

1.1 Supplies for This Unit

1. Resources used throughout

   - Stories Combo Set: *The California Coast* reader and *California Out of the Box Supplement*, available at carriershellcurriculum.com

     [The Stories Combo Set replaces the out of print *Stories from Where We Live: The California Coast* (Sara St. Antoine, ISBN 1-57131-631-0) and paperback edition *The California Coast: A Literary Field Guide (Stories from Where We Live)*, (ISBN 1-57131-653-1).]

   - *National Audubon Society Field Guide to California* (ISBN 978-0-679-44678-1)

   - *Institute for Excellence in Writing (IEW) Student Resource Notebook* (recommended, contains the List of Banned [common] Words, with great word choice alternatives, ISBN 978-1-62341042-1)

   - Composition Book

   - Sketch Book, 8x10 or smaller, with perforation for easy tearing

   - 3-Hole Pocket Folder

2. Chapter 2: *Island of the Blue Dolphins*

- *Island of the Blue Dolphins* (Scott O'Dell, ISBN 978-0-547-32861-4)

- 8x5" index cards

- Timeline: 3x5" blank index cards, 6" wide (long) banner paper, index card ring (see other Timeline options under "Timeline Introduction," section 2.5.3, page 34)

- Optional Habitat Home Building Supplies. See "Habitat Study: Coast and Islands" (section 2.2.2, page 18), for project description. (This project can be done throughout the curriculum for each of the 8 habitats.)

- Library book about sea otters for "Chapters 23-24," page 29

- Clear packing tape, 2" or wider

- Ribbon or string

- Hole punch

3. Chapter 3: Prehistory

- *Death Trap: The Story of the La Brea Tar Pits* (recommended, Sharon Elaine Thompson, ISBN 0-8225-2851-7)

1.2 Week 1

What to look for...

Symbol	Subject
	Mapwork & geography
	Habitat study
	Timeline entry
	Historical research exercise

1.2.1 Discovery

> **Big Questions** are a tool to pique student interest in an area to be considered. They can be read before or after the material. If they generate a good discussion, go with it! Don't feel you have to get to all of the reading comprehension questions. See page ix for discussion on this topic.

> Additionally, before beginning this section, be sure to build Student Folder. See page xvii for instructions.

Big Question: If we see something we have never seen before, how can we find out more about it?

Read "Seacoast Secret," in *The California Coast* reader (*Stories from Where We Live*), pages 164 to 168 (to the end of the 3rd paragraph, ending in "encyclopedia").

Read to Students Imagine you were in Tim's and Kate's place on this trip. It was you who noticed a new animal that you had never seen before. You told your friends and family, and they didn't believe you.

- What would you do? What might you feel?

- How might you discover what animal you were seeing?

Read to the end of the story on page 171.

Read to Students

- How did Kate find out what she saw? *Kate tried to find the sea otter in an encyclopedia. Not finding one, her mom suggested she write Stanford biologists, which she did, describing the animal she found and even drawing a picture.*

- How would you feel if you were in her position, meeting the scientist?

- What animals have you seen in natural environments in California?

Reflection Chart   Have students use the Animals and Habitats chart in Student Folder (table A.1 found on page 244) to remember animal sightings, and where they saw them, and in what approximate season they saw these animals. If they are having difficulty remembering encounters, have a discussion about vacations, camping trips, or hikes they have taken.

Animal	Place	Date	Season	The animal was ...

Written Reflection   Have students pick one of the animal sightings they included in table A.1. In their Composition Books, they will write a brief reflection about one of these encounters. Some things to include:

- Where they were and how they came to meet this animal?

- Was it a friendly meeting, or were they scared?

- What was the place like where they met the animal – forest, desert, or at home?

- Who else was there?

- Include a physical description of the animal.

- Using a large index card (8x5), they can include a drawing of the encounter and tape it in their Composition Book.

1.2.2 Social Studies: What Makes Me Who I Am?

Teacher's Note The focus of this curriculum is encouraging students to reflect in an honest way about the experience of others – different from their own. As they consider the lives of characters in different time periods, their perspective on their own lives will be enlarged in an organic way.

This initial exercise is intended to center students in their own experience and encourage them to dig deep.

Discuss What makes my family who we are?

1. What family members live with you?

2. Does your family have meetings with extended family? What are these meetings centered upon?

3. What routines does your family do together – i.e., shopping, sports, holidays?

4. What jobs do each of the members of your family perform?

5. If there is a conflict, how does it get resolved? Who is present, a few or everyone?

Questions paraphrased from Carmela Gomes, "Questions That Move a Discussion," September 7, 2000. Used with permission.

Model Mind Map Project for Students   A mind map, also known as a bubble map, is a graphical tool that explores connections between objects. In the middle of a blank sheet of paper, draw a circle and model the exercise for students using your own information (or a movie character, etc.) or using the students own information. See example on next page. Students can create their own on figure B.1 on page 272. Write the subject's name in the center of the middle circle. Then consider the question of **"What makes ME who I am?"** (Murdoch, 2015). Draw line segments off the center circle and connect these to more circles filled with the answers to this question. Students can answer it in terms of hobbies, location where they live or go to school, family (siblings, parents and grandparents), religion, or any other aspects they consider a part of their identity. If they are drawing a blank, it's important to model this for them. They can further divide up this second level, with lines and third order circles, even noting hobbies of their family members.

Source: Kath Murdoch, *The Power of Inquiry: Teaching and Learning with Curiosity, Creativity and Purpose in the Contemporary Classroom* (Melbourne: Seastar Publishing, 2015), 44-45. All credited questions used with permission.

Mind map example:

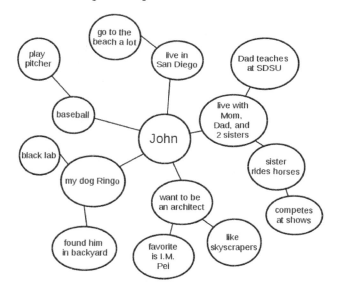

1.2.3 Looking at the Land: Map Introduction

Teacher's Note Maps reinforce the physical location of the events and stories in this curriculum. You may choose a high- or low-tech format for your students. For the low-tech approach, you will work with the maps listed in "Building Student Folder." These maps are found in the Appendix. Your students will use Google Earth to find the locations. All of the labeling will be on the maps in their Student Folder.

The back of the door becomes the map option for the California Map: Using large plain white butcher paper (five feet long piece), with a Sharpie draw an outline map of California using the California Map (figure B.2) as a template. The benefit to having a large California map is that students can take turns drawing in the various items, and you can also include photos of areas of interest. A large California map will increase the level of engagement for your students. Project source: Carmela Gomes, interview by Christine Echeverri, Pasadena, July 3, 2018.

The high-tech option involves using National Geographic Mapmaker. This program is free and web-based. No account is necessary. An adult should save the map. An e-mail address is required that generates a link that students can use to edit the map. Students may add text and label their journey through California.

```
https://mapmaker.nationalgeographic.org/
```

Read to Students To get some familiarity with the places where you see animal life, you will spend some time looking at the land of California in maps.

Big Question: What can a map tell us? (Murdoch, 2015)

Discussion and Group Work: Use the Internet to Explore Maps

1. In a computer web browser (such as Firefox or Safari) type in "Google." Click on the top listing to get to a Google search bar (blank rectangular box with a cursor blinking).

2. In a Google search bar, type in "Map of California." When you get your map, click on the box that says "satellite."

3. What surrounds California? What states and/or bodies of water do you see? *Pacific Ocean, Oregon, Mexico, Nevada, Arizona, Lake Tahoe, Salton Sea*

4. Looking at the land itself, what colors of land forms do you see? Zoom in to look at some rivers, lakes, and mountains. What are some names of forest areas, lakes, or rivers? *Some examples include: brown desert, green forested patches, and blue lakes. Some of the monuments are Sequoia National Forest, Mojave Desert, Lake Tahoe.*

5. Locate the city where you live. What other cities are close? Label your city on your California Map (figure B.2) in your Student Folder or in National Geographic Mapmaker. See note above about making a large back-of-the-door California map.

6. Using Google Earth or the inside flap of the *National Audubon Society Field Guide to California,* hereafter listed as *Audubon,* locate some of the major cities and neighbors of California. Find, mark, and label on your California Map (figure B.2, or in Mapmaker program) the following:

   - Sacramento
   - San Francisco
   - Santa Barbara
   - Monterey
   - Los Angeles
   - San Diego
   - Pacific Ocean
   - Mexico

See figure C.1 for a completed California Map Key.

7. Now, using either an online map or the *Audubon* guide, look off the coast of Santa Barbara between Santa Barbara and Los Angeles for a group of islands. What is the name of this group of islands? *Channel Islands and/or Channel Islands National Park*

8. Using the Channel Islands Map (figure B.3), fill in the names of each of the islands. *Santa Cruz, Santa Rosa, Anacapa Island, Santa Catalina, San Miguel, Santa Barbara, San Nicolas, San Clemente*

Answer key:

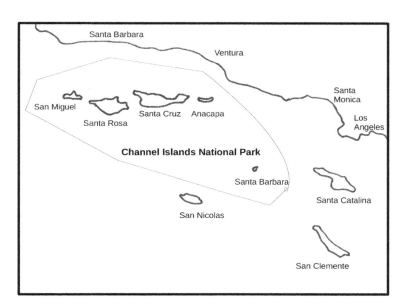

*Note, some labeling included on this map will occur later.

9. Which is the farthest north? *San Miguel or Santa Cruz*

10. Farthest south? *San Clemente*

11. Largest? *Santa Cruz*

12. Closest to the mainland? *Anacapa*

13. Farthest from the mainland? *San Nicolas*

Teacher's Note   Interestingly, there has been quite a bit of controversy surrounding water and sources of water in the state. Search Tulare Lake and Salton Sea to hear some of these fascinating stories.

Chapter 2

Island of the Blue Dolphins

2.1   Week 2

Teacher's Note   With each chapter of *Island of the Blue Dolphins*, comprehension questions (and answers) as well as big questions and reflection questions are provided.   See page ix for more information about types of questions. Feel free to use some, all, or none, as you wish. They may be used for discussion, prompts for writing to be included in the Composition Book, or have your students draw the answers in their Sketch Book. Also, in the homeschool environment, for younger siblings see "Suggestions for Younger Siblings," page xxvi.

Oral Narration Option   In lieu of the questions, you may choose to have your students give you an **oral narration** or summary of what they remember from the day's reading selection. If they draw a blank, you can ask them to tell you about the events or characters in the story. They should put their thoughts in a few complete sentences. You may choose to have them say the narration, and then (you, the teacher) write it on a white board as they say it, and they can recopy the dictation in their Composition Books. Really important to this option is that you as the teacher must be prepared that the events or parts of the story that your students remember may not be the ones that you think are important.

Often times young students will say what they think the teacher wants to hear. It is vital that you allow them to say the aspects that *they* view are important. No answers are provided for narration, as this will vary student by student.

Read to Students   You will now consider a story that occurs on one of these islands: San Nicolas Island. Using your Islands Map as a reference (figure B.3), locate and label San Nicolas Island on your California Map (figure B.2).

2.1.1   Chapters 1-4

Teacher's Note   The driving questions to consider in discussions about *Island of Blue Dolphins* are:

How does the main character, Karana, keep herself alive on the island? What resources does she use? How has she learned how to survive?

Read to Students   As you read *Island of Blue Dolphins* by Scott O'Dell, pay careful attention to the way the main character – Karana – lives. Imagine you are there with her in the story. Notice what she eats, how she builds her home, how she gets her food, and the daily challenges she faces.

Big Question: What is it that makes this place unique? (Murdoch, 2015)

1. How old are Karana and Ramo? *12 and 6, respectively.*

2. How is the island described in Chapters 1 and 2? What animals live there? What type of plants grow? *The island is shaped like a dolphin. It gets a lot of wind, so the trees grow small and twisted. There are lots of whales, sea otters, fish, orcas, bass, cormorants, and dolphins.*

3. Draw a picture of what you imagine this island might look like. You may want to have a Sketch Book out as you read Chapter 2.

4. What are the types of people (people groups) mentioned? Who were the Aleuts? (Hint: you may need to look this up). *The groups mentioned are the native villagers of Ghalas-at, the Aleuts, and Russian Captain Orlov. The Aleuts are the indigenous people from the Aleutian Islands and Western Alaska. They are closely related to the Inuits (Eskimos).*

5. Identify the "elders," the oldest members in each of the groups. *The elders are Chief Chowig and Captain Orlov.*

6. Fill in the chart for Groups on San Nicolas Island (table A.2)

Sample answers:

People group	Foods	Type of work they are doing	Nature they interact with	Weapons	Other Notes
Aleuts	*dried fish*	*hunting otters, preparing pelts sharpening spears*	*ocean, otters*	*knives, guns, spears, iron spear tips*	
Ghalas-at Villagers	*seeds, sea bass, roots*	*fishing gathering roots, making spears*	*island, land, rocky coast, bass, plants, logs*	*spears*	

Reflection In this story, the members of the tribe have a common name and a "secret, magical" name. What are Karana's two names, and which one is the secret name? If you could have a secret name, what would your name be? *Won-a-pa-lei is her common name and Karana is her secret name.*

2.1.2 Chapters 5-7

Big Question: Why do people belong to groups? (Murdoch, 2015)

1. After the battle with the Aleuts, there are many things that are lost. Make a list of the things that have changed and/or are lost. *27 villagers die, Kimki is chosen as the new chief, women must help harvest food instead of staying at home, the tribe is more serious and laughs less, new chief Kimki boards canoe for land in East and doesn't return*

2. The tribe notices that the water level in the springs is low. What does the tribe decide to do? *They decide to conserve water.*

3. **Bonus** What is this weather condition called when the water level is low? *It is called a drought.*

Reflection If you were in Karana's place, what would you do if you realized your brother was not on the boat? Have you had times when you have lost people or things? How did you feel when you realized it was lost? What did you do to retrieve it? Were you able to find what you were looking for? Write a journal entry in your Composition Book where you recount this story of something you lost.

2.2 Week 3

2.2.1 Chapters 8-9

Teacher's Note Read this box prior to chapters 8 and 9. You may explain this paragraph in your own words or read it to your students when you get to the discussion section below.

Adaptations and Consequences People occasionally cannot keep on doing what they used to do because their efforts fail at getting the outcome they want; they must come up with new ways of getting the job done. These new ways are called **adaptations** and they enable people to find new solutions to real problems. Though things used to work in a certain way, the same solution no longer works exactly the same way any more, without a consequence. A **consequence** is a positive or negative outcome that happens due to an action or inaction.

Big Question: Can anything good come from something bad?

1. In Chapter 8, Ramo and Karana begin their new life without the rest of their tribe. What are some of the challenges they face as they begin to survive without the rest of their people? *Wild dogs eat their food and now they both must work to obtain their food. Also they need a heavy canoe for fishing.*

2. In Chapter 9, after Ramo's death, Karana must begin again, this time alone. What are some of the new tasks she realizes she must do and learn? *She must defend herself from the wild dogs, make weapons, and make a new home on a rock where the dogs won't get her.*

3. What might happen if she does not make these changes? What are her biggest dangers? *She would die if she did not make these changes. Her biggest danger is being attacked by wolves. Also, since she is alone, she must be concerned each day that she has enough food.*

Discussion and Reflection: Adaptations & Consequences

1. Read or explain paragraph above (Adaptation and Consequences) to students.

2. What's an example of an adaptation from these chapters? *An example of an adaptation is Karana deciding to make weapons after Ramo dies. There had been tribal taboos (rules against) women making weapons. But since she is the only one alive, there were no more boys or men left, she decides she will need to make weapons to defend herself.*

3. Think of an example of a consequence from these chapters. *A positive consequence to her making weapons is that she will be able to ensure her safety by defending herself against the wild dogs. A negative consequence to weapon making would be if all of the taboos against women making weapons came true.*

4. Think of a few examples of adaptations that you or people in your family have had to make as a response to a situation. What was the situation? Was there a positive or negative consequence to the adaptation?

2.2.2   Habitat Study: Coast and Islands

> **Teacher's Note**   Before beginning this first Habitat Study, consider whether you will have your students fill out Habitat Description Sheets or if they will do the Native Habitat Home Building Project which is described later in this section.

Big Question: How are plants and animals the same and different? (Murdoch, 2015)

Read   the introductory paragraph on "Habitats" in *The California Coast* reader (*Stories from Where We Live*), found on page 208.

1. What is a **habitat**? *A habitat is a place where living organisms reside, eat, and find shelter. Outside of that habitat, the same plant or animal might not survive.*

2. What life forms do habitats include? *plants and animals*

3. What are some habitats you have heard of or been to?

   Read   the "Rocky Shore, Sea Cliffs, Sandy Beach and Dune, and Channel Islands" in *The California Coast* reader (*Stories from Where We Live*), pages 208-211. Also, in *Audubon*, read "Coastal and Island Habitats," pages 36-37.

   Big Question: Why do living things protect themselves?

4. What are the names of the 5 tidal zones found on rocky coastlines? *subtidal, low intertidal, middle intertidal, high intertidal, splash zone*

5. Between the sea cliffs, sandy beaches, and Channel Islands, which habitat has the most diversity of life, and why? *The Channel Islands do, as more plants and animals are found there.*

6. What are some of the adaptations of the plants and animals to the conditions found in these habitats? *Some examples include the common murre bird, which lays its highly tapered-shaped eggs on narrow ledges, spy island gray foxes that climb trees and dune plants that keep sand dunes anchored.*

7. Fill out Habitat Tracker A (table A.3) for Coast and Island habitats.

8. For the location box for each habitat, see the back flap of the *Audubon* guide for a map of the habitats. Using this map, find cities for each habitat.

9. Below is a key for this habitat. See section C.1, page 295 for key with all habitats.

Habitat	Trees/Shrubs	Flowering Plants	Animals	Location (cities)
Coast & Islands	*Surf grass eel grass, giant kelp bed (Santa Rosa Island), Channel Island trees (3 types)*	*Beach primrose, beach morning glory, sea palm, angelica*	*Western gulls, humpback whales, California sea lion, sea anemonies, acorn barnacles*	*San Diego, Monterey, Ventura, Santa Barbara, Mendocino, Long Beach, Carlsbad*

Substitute Project: Native Habitat Home Building Design

An option to filling out a Habitat Description for each habitat section (listed in the next step) is to create a home made of

> the materials, rocks, and plants found in each of the 8 habitats students study. This project is recommended for independent and non-traditional learners. After reading each section, look for photos of the habitat and of Native American's housing. For brainstorming purposes, ask your students to make a list of materials they notice in photos and while reading stories about this habitat in their Composition Books. Their houses do not have to look like a structure created by a known tribe, but they should be made only of natural items that are found in that habitat.
>
> Take a photo of each structure and have students affix photos in their Sketch Books. At the top of each page, label the page for that habitat. Have students write a few sentences about the materials they chose.

10. Locate the Habitat Description page (table A.5). Label the habitat "Coast and Island Habitats." Use the *Audubon* guide and Google Images to search California for pictures from this habitat (Google search terms: california coast and islands habitats photos). Draw a picture from one of these areas, showing the land, a plant, and an animal. Label each of these features you include. Write a few sentences about the habitat.

> *Sample habitat description: The coast and islands habitat is home to many animals that have adapted to living in rocky areas, and plants that can live with very little fresh water. Most of the animals must deal with the impacts of high surf. One example is the sea otter wrapping itself in kelp to stay anchored while feeding. On the sand dunes there are beach plants such as beach primrose and beach morning glory, and animals such as ghost shrimp and pacific sand crabs.*

2.2.3   Chapters 10-12

Big Question: What makes us happy? (Murdoch, 2015)

1. What natural life on the island makes Karana happy and feel less afraid? *stars, gulls, dolphins, otters, and white rings of foam around the rocks*

2. As she fixes her canoe, what are some materials she adapts make the canoe usable to her? What is pitch? (Hint: you may need to look it up using Google search terms: pitch-resin).
   She fixes her canoe with pitch and fiber from her skirt. Pitch is natural asphalt or tar that washes up on the beach. Native people heated it and used it to line baskets and boats to waterproof them.

3. What natural materials does she use to build her house? How does she fashion the different elements? Draw a picture of what you envision her house to look like.
   She uses kelp, whale bones, wood, and sinew. She builds a fence with whale bones wrapped with kelp, pointed outward to keep foxes and dogs away. She constructs the house by erecting the poles, tying them with sinew and wrapping them with kelp.

4. **Bonus** In Chapter 12, she builds her house and cooks; what are some adaptations she has made – what does she do differently than her tribe?
   She is able to save fish juice, save her fire each night so she doesn't need to start it anew each day, and she makes rock shelves in her house to keep the mice away.

2.2.4   Science: Plant Observation & Collection

Big Question: What can we learn from field trips?

Choose Field Trip Location   Visit a natural area and walk quietly among the plants. If possible, visit an area like a canyon, a beach, or other unimproved area. Choose a location where the vegetation is not watered with sprinklers or tended to by gardeners. This type of environment will give your students an idea of how the area grows apart from human involvement. If visiting a state or national park, be aware of the laws surrounding collecting objects and do not violate the laws.

Materials:

- Large ziplock bag for field trip

- Large index cards (8x5)

- Clear packing tape

- Hole punch

- Yarn or ribbon

On Field Trip: Collection of Samples and Discussion

1. Take 5-10 samples of plants, flowers, and/or leaves, putting them in a large ziplock bag.

2. What types of plants and trees do you see?

3. Which plant do you like the best?

Create Collection   Lay each sample down on a large index card. Using thick, clear packing tape, spread the sample out, fanning and facing the leaves up, so it can be observed how the leaves connect to the stem. Tape each plant down, taking care to remove air pockets in the tape around the plant, so that each plant is completely covered by tape.

Starting at 1, number each sample card. Write the location and the date collected.

Read to Students   Trees, leaves, flowers, and plants can be shaped in many ways. There is a language to describe them. They may be placed in categories with common characteristics which aid in identification.

Observation & Identification Have students use *Audubon* to fill out the Leaf Observation chart (table A.6), as it applies to each sample. Some boxes may not apply and may remain blank.

Use these *Audubon* sections to identify leaf and flower types and shapes:

- Fern Frond Types, page 93

- Trees, page 96

- Leaf Shapes, page 132

- Leaf Arrangements, page 132

- Flower Types, page 133

- Flower Cluster Types, page 133

In the last column, using the field guide, have students make a guess as to which plants they found. Explore the following sections in *Audubon* for identification: Lichen, Trees and Shrubs, Broadleaf Trees and Shrubs, and Wildflowers. *See sample chart below.*

Sample Number	Tree Shape	Leaf Shape	Leaf Arrange-ment	Flower Type	Flower Cluster Type	Identi-fication
1		*Needles in cluster*	*Opposite*			*Rosemary*
2		*Linear*	*Sheathing*			*Grass*

Bind Collection Book Have students design covers for their collections with a title and their name. The Leaf Observation Table can be added to the book by gluing it on a card at the end. Bind all cards together by punching 2-3 holes in the left side, and tie together with yarn or ribbon.

2.3   Week 4

2.3.1   Chapters 13-15

Big Question: What makes a good pet and why do people have them? (Murdoch, 2015)

1. How would you describe how Karana feels about spearing the elephant seal bull? What qualities make them hard to kill? Why does she feel skeptical of her ability to kill it?
   She feels overwhelmed and scared to kill the bull. The seals are large, angered easily, and often fight with each other. She's is worried that because she (a woman) made her own weapon, it will fail when she needs to use it.

2. What does she do to help heal the injury she received from trying to kill the bull? *She remains in her house for five days. When she needs to get water, she crawls to the ravine and she stays in another cave for six days.*

3. Draw a picture of what you think the cave looks like where she hides after her injury. What does she decide a good use for this cave might be? *She makes a second home in this cave her ancestors used; she makes a bed, stores food, firewood, and old weapons.*

4. After she deals with the wild dogs, Rontu finds himself in a new home. How does he, a wild dog, come to live with Karana? *She almost killed him. When she comes back and finds him and points her arrow at him, he does not run. She begins to take care of him.*

5. How does he become her pet? *She carries him to her house, leaves him there and sets out food and water for him. She sleeps elsewhere until she is sure it's safe to sleep in her house with him.*

2.3.2 Poetry: Reading & Project

Teacher's Note Before reading the poetry selections that follow, either read these two paragraphs to students or explain these ideas in your own words. Brainstorm with students 1-3 examples of each.

Personification One device commonly used in poetry is **personification**, where a nonhuman object is given human qualities or attributes. For example, "The wind danced over the sand dune."

Simile Another device is **simile**. This concept is very similar to metaphor, but the words "like" and "as" are used. An example is, "The pine tree was as tall as a skyscraper." The comparison is between a pine tree and a skyscraper. Note: metaphors will be discussed in "Introduction to Unit V Projects" on page 199.

Read "The Poppy" (page 193), "The Dolphins" (page 185), and "Ode to a Plain Old Pond Frog" (page 195) in *The California Coast* reader (*Stories from Where We Live*).

Big Question: How can words paint a picture? (Murdoch, 2015)

- As you read, have your students listen for examples of personification and simile. Reread as necessary to generate examples.

- Share one personification and one simile from these poems. *An example of personification is the phrase "boat stepped" in "The Dolphins." An example of simile in "The Poppy" is where the petals of a poppy are said to be "like" the wings of a monochrome moth.*

Project Students will begin work on poems of their own about their favorite plant, tree, or flower in California. They may write in their Composition Books or on a computer. Use the *IEW SRN List of Banned Words* for great lists of words to replace (boring) common words.

Before students write, have them read more about their flower or plant in *Audubon*, or in another reference.

In their Composition Books, have them brainstorm 4-6 phrases using personification or similes for their chosen plant. *Example: The edges of oak tree leaves are as sharp as a pair of scissors.*

A simple poetry form is the Acrostic Poem. Students can choose a word, and with each letter of that particular letter of the chosen word, written vertically, they will find unique adjectives to describe the plant. For example:

P leasant
I mmense
N ice, neat needles
E xpansive

Other poetry forms are possible if you have already studied them in your writing curriculum.

Students should give their poems a title, and they should write their name and the date under the title. They can also add a drawing to embellish their poems.

2.3.3   Chapters 16-17

Big Question: Why change the ways we do things?

1. Have students finish their poems.

2. What are some ways Karana modifies the canoe that belonged to her tribe? *She decides to make it smaller by loosening the planks and cutting the sinew, heating pitch, and trimming the wood planks with a stone knife she found.*

3. What does she remember and find when she finds the large black cave? *She remembers the two ancestral gods Tumaiyowit and Murkat, she sees a devilfish (octopus), and she finds a place to hide her canoe.*

Reflection Rontu gets in a fight with the wild dogs. Karana decides not to intervene, as she thinks he will get in a fight again at a time and place where Rontu might lose if he doesn't solve the situation right then and there. If you were in her position, would you have made the same choice, or not? Have you been in situations where you, like Rontu, had to solve something in that moment, or the situation would happen again?

2.3.4 Mythology: The Earth Dragon

Read to Students The large cave reminds Karana of the two ancestral gods Tumaiyowit and Murkat. Many Native Americans have stories called myths which explain how things were created or how things work.

Big Question: What can myths teach us? (Murdoch, 2015)

Read "The Earth Dragon" (See *California Out of the Box Supplement* for story location. Appeared originally in *Stories from Where We Live*, page 92.)

Draw or illustrate a part of this story.

2.3.5 Chapters 18-19

Big Question: How are humans and animals connected? (Murdoch, 2015)

1. How does Karana tame her 2 birds? *She takes them out of their nest, they live in a cage in her house, she clips their wings, and she feeds them out of her hand.*

2. She finally kills the devilfish. Why might she decide to forgo killing the other 2 devilfish she sees that summer? *In the process of killing the octopus, it attacks both her and Rontu.*

3. What are some of the items she makes in these chapters? What does she use to make them? *She makes: a skirt of yucca twine, a belt and*

sandals of seal skin and a flower wreath for her and Rontu. She gets purple dye from sea urchins.

4. Humans and animals must procure food. What are some ways Karana and other animals harvest food in these chapters? *Karana harvests red abalone and spears a devilfish; starfish eat red abalone; seagulls eat scallops.*

2.4 Week 5

2.4.1 Chapters 20-22

Big Question: Where do words come from? (Murdoch, 2015)

In Chapter 20, Karana discovers Black Cave. She sees remnants of her ancestors. Due to the tide, she gets stuck and must stay there overnight.

1. Put yourself in Karana's place. Imagine you see a bird fly out of a space and discover a deep cave. Write a short paragraph, draw a picture, or make a model of the cave you found. What does it look like inside? Are there particular objects inside? Is there wildlife? What does it feel like to be inside?

2. Karana sees the Aleuts return. Because she is fearful, she packs baskets of her most important items each time she moves her home. What does she include, and why might she include these items? *She takes her 2 birds, yucca skirt, utensils she made, beads and earrings, baskets, weapons, and cormorant feathers. She takes these items because it would take her a lot of time to replace them and/or build them anew.*

3. If you were in a situation in which you had to leave your home quickly, what would you try to rescue at the last minute? What significance do these items hold for you?

4. She and Tutok eventually get along well. They have fun exchanging words with each other in their native language. In table A.7, choose 5 English words, and then find their meaning in a language of your choice, preferably one that is new to you, using a language dictionary. Say them aloud. Do they sound similar, or very different?

2.4.2 Chapters 23-24

Read to Students Before reading *Island of the Blue Dolphins*, you read the story about Kate, who discovered that sea otters were making a comeback off the California coast (section 1.2.1, page 4). *Island of the Blue Dolphins* gives the context for how they were hunted initially by fur trappers.

Big Question: What can we learn from sea otters?

1. Briefly research sea otters. Read "There Oughter Be an Otter" in *The California Coast* reader (*Stories from Where We Live*) for more information on how otters live (page 197), as well as briefly consulting other library and/or online references.

2. Have students brainstorm information they have learned about otters. From this information, they should write 1-3 paragraphs. They can discuss where otters geographically live, how they eat, and their family structure. Students should cover why they were almost hunted to extinction.

Sample paragraphs: Sea otters use tools such as rocks to help them crack open shellfish. They must be quick as they have to fight off gulls. To anchor while eating and sleeping, they wrap their bodies in kelp. They do not migrate. They live in the same geographic area close to the shoreline their whole lives, breeding and tending to their young.

One reason they were almost hunted to extinction is their dense fur, which has on average 500,000 hairs per square inch. They also have a layer of air between their skin and their pelt which insulates them. These two features allow them to stay in the same area instead of migrating as other marine mammals must do. They now live off the coast of California from Half Moon Bay in the north to Santa Barbara in the south.

Reflection In Chapter 24, Karana has changed her views on animals. To her, animals have become like people – friends to her. She cannot imagine hunting most of them anymore. Imagine you are living in her place, existing on this island by yourself. How might you feel towards animals? What particular animals from the story so far would you feel closest to?

2.4.3 Chapters 25-26

Big Question: What happens when we lose something we love?

Reflection   In these chapters, Karana loses Rontu.

1. How would you feel if you were in Karana's place? If you were Karana, what would you miss about Rontu?

2. Ask your students if they have lost a pet, friend, or family member.

3. In their Sketch Books, have them draw the people or pets they lost.

4. Have students write a 1-paragraph story in their Composition Books about something their lost loved one did that was meaningful to them. It could be some mischief that he or she got into, or a funny story about their family member, etc.

5. Have any students experienced a pet's death? How did they bury their pet or loved one? Did they bury them with anything, or add any decorations to the grave? Why did they choose those decorations? Have them write 1-paragraph answering these questions.

2.4.4 Chapters 27-28

In these 2 chapters, a powerful tsunami and earthquake hit the island. Karana paints a vivid picture of how things change.

Big Question: How are living things connected? (Murdoch, 2015)

1. Look at Google Images for photos of tsunami waves. **Google search terms: tsunami wave photos**

2. Have students draw a picture from the story of either the tsunami or earthquake.

3. What are some jobs Karana does after the earthquake to rebuild? *After the storm, she takes inventory of everything. She decides to fashion a new canoe.*

4. In Google Images, look for a picture of Hokusai's famous woodblock print, *Great Wave Off Kanagawa*.

5. Briefly research and write a paragraph about how a tsunami works. Visit these sites:

   `http://academic.evergreen.edu/g/grossmaz/springle/`

   or

   `https://walrus.wr.usgs.gov/tsunami/.`

   Sample paragraph: Tsunamis result from seismic activity such as earthquakes on the Earth's crust under the ocean. When the earth rises or falls as the plates move together, large waves are formed in the ocean, and can travel quickly and unpredictably. These waves can last for hours. Most tsunamis happen along the ring of fire in the Pacific Ocean, especially along the coast of Japan.

2.5 Week 6

2.5.1 Chapter 29

Big Question: Imagine you, like Karana, had to leave your home. What is worth saving? (Murdoch, 2015)

1. What does Karana do when the men come to the island? *She watches them, begins preparations to leave the island, builds a fire, cooks a meal, paints her face, and puts her cormorant outfit on.*

2. What items and animals does she gather to leave the island? *She takes her otter cape, cormorant skirt, black earrings and black necklace, Rontu-Aru, and her birds.*

3. How does Karana feel about wearing the clothing the men made for her? How is the dress different from what she has been wearing? *The men make her a blue dress. She doesn't like it as it's hot and scratchy.*

4. How does she responds to the men who ask if there are otters around there? *She pretends she cannot understand them.*

5. How long do you estimate she lived on the island? *Answers will vary. She actually lived there 18 years.*

Reflection Put yourself in Karana's place. How would you feel as you left the island? Would you be glad, sad, or something else? What things might you miss?

2.5.2   History: The Lone Woman

Big Question: Why read fiction? (Murdoch, 2015)

Read to Students *Island of the Blue Dolphins* is a work of historical fiction, which means it has been researched, but liberties have been added to the story by the author to fill out details. Not everything can be known about her daily life on the island. To get an idea of what is historically known about Karana, read "The Lone Woman of San Nicolas Island," in *The California Coast* reader (*Stories from Where We Live*), page 147. Complete table A.8 with some of the known facts.

Big Question: Can we belong to more than one culture?

1. Year that 18 Native Americans were brought from the island to mainland CA: <u>1835</u>

2. The people who wanted the Native Americans taken to the mainland were the <u>Mission Fathers</u>

3. Number of years it is estimated that the "lone woman" lived on the island alone: <u>18</u>

4. They think she may have dived off the boat to rescue her <u>child</u>

5. The type of clothing she wore:
   <u>cormorant feather dress with sinew rope</u>

6. Nature that she could silence: <u>wind</u>

7. The name of the tribe she was a part of:
   <u>Nicoleño Indians, Gha-las-hat village</u>

8. Name of the captain who rescued her: <u>George Nidever</u>

9. Year she was rescued: <u>1853</u>

10. Number of weeks she lived after being rescued: <u>7 weeks</u>

11. Reasons they think she died: <u>change of diet or germs</u>

12. When she was rescued, how was she able to communicate?
    <u>hand and facial gestures</u>

13. Mission where she is buried: <u>Santa Barbara</u>

14. The name they gave to her: <u>Juana Maria</u>

2.5.3   Timeline Introduction

Teacher's Note As your students work through the curriculum, you will see events that are both historical and personal in nature for them to add to a timeline. These will be listed in a box, like the section that follows. Similarly to the map formatting options, there are 2 choices for creating a timeline: a high-tech and a low- tech approach.

The low-tech approach involves placing timeline events on 3x5 (blank) index cards and arranging them in order at the end of the curriculum on a long piece of scroll paper. As students work through the curriculum, have them title each card with the historical date and an event name. They can draw pictures to illustrate. To help keep their cards organized, punch holes in the top left corner and keep them in chronological order with a index card ring. Events will be added throughout the curriculum, non-linearly.

The high-tech approach involves signing up for a free account at Timetoast, an easy-to-use timeline creator. The advantage of this is that your students may upload photos for their events, save their timelines as they go, and print them out when completed. Important: an adult must sign-up for the account.

    https://www.timetoast.com/

Add to Timeline

Have students add these dates in desired Timeline format.

- Year the Nicoleño Indians left San Nicolas Island: _1835_

- Year Karana was rescued: *1853*

2.5.4 Historical Research: Overview

Teacher's Note Another thread which can be introduced to your students if you have not yet covered it is how to do research – and the importance of consideration of a variety of sources. These research sections are woven throughout the curriculum. After you read this list below to students, have students come up with 1-3 examples of each source.

Big Question: How do we know if something is true? (Murdoch, 2015)

Read to Students It is valuable to consider the types of sources one can use to understand how people in the past lived. Here are some important reference categories:

- **Primary Sources** originate in the time period being studied. Examples include the *Declaration of Independence* and the *Magna Carta*. Also, writing such as oral histories and journal entries are primary sources. These sources reflect how people thought and lived in that historical time. *Example: The Diary of Anne Frank*

- **Secondary Sources** are resources that use primary sources to craft a narrative about a time period. They are often written after the time period, and contain opinions and new ways to look at the time period. They are subject to more interpretation as authors craft what they believe the story of the past to be. *Examples: Story of the World, various textbooks*

- **Fiction** books and resources are not factual. They depart from reality in various ways. They are not based on the actual events of a person's life. An author may create situations that a certain type of person *might* have done. Most detective stories and fantasy books are fictional. *Examples: The Lord of the Rings, The Hobbit, Nancy Drew, and Hardy Boys*

- **Nonfiction** books rely on information that can be proven. Many science, math, history books, and biographies are classified as nonfiction. They present information that can be verified. Nonfiction historical authors use primary sources to research their books, and then are limited to only work with the facts they've learned from those sources. They cannot embellish the stories to add details. *Examples: Kingfisher Encyclopedia, books about spiders and birds (and other plants and animals)*

Have students complete table A.9 with conclusions on these resources.

Types of Sources

Source	Primary or Secondary?	Fiction or Nonfiction?
Newspaper article about California becoming a state, written in 1850	*Primary*	*Nonfiction*
Island of the Blue Dolphins	*Secondary*	*Fiction*
Native American's oral history about his or her tribal traditions	*Primary*	*Nonfiction*
A book about California history written in 2015	*Secondary*	*Nonfiction*
Captain Nidever's journal	*Primary*	*Nonfiction*

Later in this curriculum students will look more closely at primary sources.

Discuss

1. Why is it important to look at primary sources? *They give the most honest, unfiltered look at attitudes in a given period.*

2. What might primary sources tell you that a secondary source would not be able to convey? *Primary sources give the best window into what people actually thought at a specific time.*

3. What are some of the advantages to secondary sources? *Secondary sources can be easier to read. The language might be more modern. They also contain more opinions about patterns and trends about the time period, which can be interesting.*

Bonus For *Island of the Blue Dolphins*, how might Scott O'Dell have researched this story? What sources might he have used? Read the Author's Note in *Island of the Blue Dolphins* to find out more about the author's choices.

Sample answer: He considered the records of Captain Hubbard, Captain Nidever, and Father Gonzales of Santa Barbara. He also worked with researchers at the Southwest Museum and the San Diego Museum of Man. To get a better idea of what the island is like, he might have also visited the island.

Chapter 3

Prehistory

3.0.1 Poetry Reflection: Time

Read and Discuss the "Night Beach Poem," in *The California Coast* reader (*Stories from Where We Live*), page 90.

Big Question: How do the words in this poem make you feel? (Murdoch, 2015)

In this poem, the author remembers some childhood memories that include his family members. What memories does he recount? *his father swimming to the buoy when he was nine years old and his grandfather chanting while counting ants*

Written Reflection Have students brainstorm family memories. They should write a paragraph about a memory of an experience with a grandparent, other older adult, or their first memory.

To help them brainstorm, help them consider: Where were they? What was the place like? How old were they? Time of day?

Add to Timeline

- Date of this family memory, and label it. *Answers will vary.*

3.0.2   Pygmy Mammoths

Teacher's Note   Beginning in this section, your students will move from studying a Native American experience in California to going back in time to study prehistoric life. This section is not an in-depth study of mammoths, etc., but is intended to briefly touch on this period through web-based research and videos.

Read to Students   After spending time reading about what the life of a Native Californian girl might have been like, we will step back even further in time, to consider life that was here even before humans. We will stay in the Channel Islands.

Big Question: Who was here first, and how do we know? (Murdoch, 2015)

Have students look at their Channel Islands Map, (figure B.3). Have students locate the islands of Santa Rosa and Santa Catalina. Among the 8 Channel Islands, there are 5 that are a part of the Channel Islands National Park. Look them up on the web or on the map on the front inside flap of *Audubon* and circle the 5 on figure B.3. Use **Google search terms: california channel islands national park.** *Anacapa, Santa Rosa, San Miguel, Santa Cruz, Santa Barbara*

See "Looking at the Land: Map Introduction" for a Channel Islands Map key (section 1.2.3, beginning on page 9).

On the California Map (figure B.2), label Santa Rosa, Santa Catalina, and put a circle around and label the Channel Islands National Park. See figure C.1 for completed California Map Key.

Read to Students   You will now learn about an animal that was recently discovered on the island of Santa Rosa.

Look at the National Park Service Website, Channel Islands National Park, under Pygmy Mammoth.

`https://www.nps.gov/chis/learn/historyculture/pygmymammoth.htm`

Watch "Pygmy Mammoth: Life and Times."

Discussion   Make a list on a white board or in Composition Books with some important details about the pygmy mammoth. Include the following:

1. Why might the pygmy mammoths have come to the island initially? *in search of food*

2. The name of the island the pygmy mammoth swam to: *Santa Rosae*

3. What bodily features enabled it to come to the island? *it's snorkel-like trunk and bouyant body type*

4. How did the island change over time? *The island became grazed and smaller in size as the waters rose.*

5. What caused this change? *melting glaciers*

6. How did the mygmy mammoths physically change as the island changed? *They became smaller.*

7. How many years ago do scientists think this animal died? *12,800 years ago*

8. When did most other large mammoths go extinct? *10,000 years ago*

9. When was this skeleton discovered? *1994*

10. What is notable about this skeleton? *It is one of the most complete pygmy mammoth skeletons ever found.*

Writing   From these facts, have students write a brief paragraph about the Santa Rosa pygmy mammoth in their Composition Books.

Add to Timeline

- Approximate year Santa Rosa pygmy mammoth died. Hint: this year will be in BC. *10,800 BC or 12,800 years ago*

- Year mammoth skeleton was discovered *1994*

More Information

Teacher's Note   If you or your students would like more information, there are good *LA Times* articles available online about this pygmy mammoth.

Additionally, on the National Park Services site, watch "Pygmy Mammoth: Humans and Mammoths." This video has a good overview on the relationship between these animals and humans, as well as global areas where mammoths have been found.

For the excavation details, there are 4 excellent videos which fill out the discovery, also on the NPS Pygmy Mammoth website.

3.1   Week 7

3.1.1   History: Santa Catalina Island

Big Question: How do animals help humans?

Read   "Catalina's Pigeon Express." Link to this selection found in *California Out of the Box Supplement*. Originally printed in *Stories from Where We Live*, page 129.

1. During what years did the Pigeon Express operate? Why did it stop operating? *It operated between 1894-1898. It ended with the invention of wireless communication.*

2. Use Google Maps, satellite mode, to locate Santa Catalina Island (Catalina Island) and the city of Los Angeles.

3. Use Google Images to look at the route of the Pigeon Courier Service, some of the archived notes, as well as some pictures of the famous pigeons. Google search terms: pigeon courier express 1894 catalina island photos

---

Add to Timeline

- Pigeon Express dates *1894-1898*

3.1.2 Linking Time: Hollywood and the Pits

Teacher's Note The following story is about a 16-year-old girl reflecting back on her life as a child actress. While not inappropriate, it will probably be understood best by 4th-6th graders. With younger students, you may move to discussing the Tar Pits directly.

Read to Students You will now travel with the Pigeon Express to the city of Los Angeles. Within this city, you will go to the area of Hollywood.

Use Google Maps, satellite filter, to locate Hollywood. **Google search terms: los angeles hollywood map**

Read "Hollywood and the Pits," in *The California Coast* reader (*Stories from Where We Live*), page 67.

Big Question: How do places change over time? (Murdoch, 2015)

1. What job did the author do when she was young? *She was a child actress.*

2. How did things change when she was 16? *When she finally had a growth spurt, her acting work dried up because she did not look like a cute young child anymore.*

3. How has the author adapted to no longer working as an actress? *She volunteers at the La Brea Tar Pits digging up bones during summers.*

4. While working at the Tar Pits, do you think she suffered positive or negative consequences due to her adaptation? *Positive consequences – she seems pleased that she is now volunteering to discover bones.*

5. What do you learn about the Tar Pits in this story? What is this tar liquid made of? How did animals become trapped? What types of

animals were found here?

The Tar Pits are large ponds of tar that trapped animals 10,000 years ago and beyond. The animals, mostly carnivores, came to these ponds to get a drink of water, and ended up getting stuck. Other animals, thinking they would eat the shrieking victims, rushed into the tar and also got stuck. Saber-toothed cats, dire wolves, vultures, and coyote bones all mixed together as the tar moved around.

Prehistory: Discovering the Tar Pits

Big Question: How do living things change over time? (Murdoch, 2015)

1. Locate the La Brea Tar Pits on Google Maps. **Google search terms: map la brea tar pits**

2. For a good overview watch:

   La Brea Tar Pits: An Urban Mystery. Winner Bronze Telly Award 2012. By Michael Edelstein (6 minutes).

   `https://www.youtube.com/watch?v=G7FK59waeo0`

3. Use Google Images to find pictures of animals caught in the pits. **Google search terms: la brea tar pits animal photos**

4. Consult one of these sources:

   - *Audubon* pages 23-25.
   - *Death Trap: The Story of the La Brea Tar Pits* by Sharon Thompson
   - Page Museum website, under "Resources for Teachers:"

     `http://www.tarpits.org/sites/default/files/pdfs/ return%20to%20the%20ice%20age.pdf.`

5. Using table A.10 (Animals: Pleistocene vs. Modern), have students make a list of some of their favorite Pleistocene animals. Then, for comparison, students should list animals they are similar to today. Have

them make a note of how they look different today. Sample chart provided below.

Pleistocene Animal	Modern Animal Equivalent	How are the two different?
Saber-toothed cat	*Mountain lion*	*Lions don't have tusks*
Dire wolf	*Coyote*	*Dire wolf has more of a ruff of fur around face*
Colombian mammoth	*Elephant*	*Mammoths were more reddish and had more fur*
Short-faced bears	*Grizzly bear*	*Grizzly bear was much bigger*
Ground sloth	*Rainforest sloth*	*Rainforest sloths are much smaller today*
American camel	*African camel*	*American camel had only one hump, with a fur cluster on it*
American horse	*Quarter horse*	*American horse had light zebra stripes*

Add to Timeline

- The Pleistocene epoch *1.7 million to 10,000 years ago*

Source: *Death Trap: The Story of the La Brea Tar Pits* by Sharon Thompson

3.1.3   Habitat Study: Chaparral, Coastal Scrub, and Oak Woodlands

Read to Students   The area of the Tar Pits is situated in the chaparral habitat.

Big Question: What natural cycles keep habitats working?

Read   "Fire in the Chaparral!" in *The California Coast* reader (*Stories from Where We Live*), page 98.

1. What animals and trees and plants are mentioned in this story? Make a list with students.
   Trees and plants include: oak trees, manzanita and toyon bushes, sycamores, sage, willows, buckwheat, ceanothus, purple lupine, orange poppies, rich clover, and monkeyflowers. Animals include: snakes, squirrels, mule deer, hawks, lizards, mouse, rabbit, and grasshoppers.

2. How have plants adapted to "using fire" and what benefits does the fire perform in this habitat?
   Plant adaptations: branches have an oily resin that burns very hot; roots are underground and survive the fire; oak trees have fireproof bark; some seeds need fire to open. Fire benefits: acorns with damaging moths are burned; ash nourishes plants; large wildflower harvests are produced after fire.

3. From the list above, use Google Images to look up some of the plants mentioned in the chaparral. Have students pick one plant or tree to draw in their Sketch Books. Label the plant. **Google search terms: california chaparral plant photos**

   Read   "Oak Woodlands," "Chaparral," and "Coastal Scrub" sections, in *The California Coast* reader (*Stories from Where We Live*), pages 212-214.

   Also read   in *Audubon*, "Chaparral and Coastal Scrub," pages 44-45, and "Foothill Oak Woodlands," page 46.

4. What is the most dominant shaping force in the chaparral? *fire*

5. What fruit/resource in the oak woodlands was/is the most significant foodsource for both Native Americans and birds and animals in this community? *acorns*

6. In Google Images, look for some pictures of the chaparral and oak woodlands. How does the chaparral look different from the oak woodlands? **Google search terms: california chaparral photos, california oak woodland photos**
   The chaparral have patches of low-and medium-sized shrubs, but no trees. The oak woodlands have trees and grasses, but not many shrubs.

7. What colors of plants, trees, and shrubs do you see? *brown/golden grasses, yellow, purple and orange hills with wildflowers, silver and olive green shrubs, and dark green trees*

Complete Habitat Tracker A (table A.3) for Chaparral and Coastal Scrub (combining them), and one for Oak Woodlands.

Habitat	Trees/Shrubs	Flowering Plants	Animals	Location (cities)
Chaparral & Coastal Scrub	*Not many trees, but shrubs such as toyon, scrub oak, ceanothus sagebrush, buckwheat*	*Mariposa lilies, fire poppies, monkeyflowers*	*Brush rabbit, coast horned lizard, hawks, kangaroo rats*	*Monterey, Palos Verdes, San Diego, Santa Monica, Morro Bay*
Oak Woodlands	*20 species of oaks, digger pines, low shrubs like poison oak, California walnut*	*Flowering shrubs such as buckeye and squaw bush*	*Acorn woodpeckers, scrub jays, gray squirrel, mule deer*	*San Luis Obispo, Paso Robles, Coloma, Mariposa*

Fill out one Habitat Description Sheet (table A.5) for chaparral and coastal scrub (combining them) and one for oak Woodlands. Draw a picture of the land, a plant, and an animal and label them. Write a short paragraph about each habitat. You may substitute the Native Habitat Home Building Project for these 2 habitats. Project introduced in Habitat Study: Coast and Islands, beginning on page 18.

Sample paragraphs:

Chaparral and coastal scrub: The chaparral is composed of hardy evergreen shrubs that are dependent on fire to thin. Over time the environment becomes dense. The trees have a oil in their bark, which helps them to burn fast. The coastal scrub is similar, but shrubs are even smaller, and much of the plant growth remains under the soil. Many of these plants grow only during the cool wet winters, as they get very low rainfall during other parts of the year. During the summer, many coastal scrub plants drop their leaves to avoid drying out.

Oak woodlands: The oak woodlands are found in the foothills of California mountain ranges. They are found more inland than in the chaparral. Most of the trees are deciduous oak trees and pines that are highly drought tolerant. One of the sustaining features of this habitat are acorns. Many birds and squirrels hide nuts to nourish themselves during winter, inadvertently planting new trees in the process.

3.1.4   Geologic Time: Going from Mammoths Further Back to Dinosaurs

---

Teacher's Note   This section concludes the look at prehistory.

Have students use Google Images to find a Geologic Time Chart. Here is a link to an creative one by Ray Troll:

Google search terms: geologic time chart ray troll

http://www.trollart.com/fossils1.html/

Have students print it out and put it in their Student Folder.

Big Question: How have plants and animals changed over time?

Discussion   Looking at the chart:

1. The period labels are written horizontally. During which 3 periods did the dinosaurs live? Hint: students may need to look this up online. *Triassic, Jurassic, Cretaceous*

2. The era labels are written vertically. In what era were the dinosaurs alive? *Mesozoic*

3. What epoch are we living in now (horizontal label)? *Holocene*

4. What era are we living in now? *Cenozoic*

5. How long ago was the Earth formed? *4.6 billion years ago*

Add to Timeline

- The Earth was formed *4.6 billion years ago*

3.1.5   End of Unit I Questions

These questions are combined with unit II/part 2 on page 90 in "End of *Antiguo* Questions (Units I & II)."

Unit II

Antiguo

(Ancient, Former)

Part 2: Missions and Ranchos

Chapter 4

Unit Introduction

4.1 Supplies for This Unit

1. Resources used throughout

   - See list on page 2

2. Chapter 5: *Valley of the Moon*

   - *Valley of the Moon: The Diary of María Rosalia de Milagros* (Sherry Garland, ISBN 0-439-08820-8)

   - *A Gift For Abuelita* (recommended [see page 66 for more information], Nancy Luenn, ISBN 0-87358-688-3)

   - *Pedro: The Angel of Olvera Street* (recommended, Leo Politi, ISBN 978-0-89236-990-4)

   - *The California Missions Sourcebook* (recommended, if available from library for section 5.4.1, beginning on page 73, David J. McLaughlin with Rubén G. Mendoza)

   - Various project supplies for "Symbolism & Remembering Our Loved Ones," page 67

   - Optional piñata making supplies for "Religious Traditions: *Las Posadas*," page 71

   - Optional Habitat Home Building Supplies. See "Habitat Study: Coast and Islands" (section 2.2.2, page 18) for project description.

Chapter 5

Valley of the Moon

5.1 Week 8

5.1.1 Research: Using the *Audubon* Guide

Teacher's Note Your students have already used the *Audubon Field Guide to California.* In this exercise, your students will explore more deeply the content in this resource. This exercise is important because students often become overwhelmed trying to find information. A simple walk through this guide when the students are not under research pressure will give them a bearing about where types of information such as the index can be found. This information is especially relevant for report writing. If you have already covered use of reference materials in your writing curriculum, feel free to move on. Have students use table A.11 to fill in the following information.

Big Question: How can we use nonfiction to be better researchers? (Murdoch, 2015)

Read to Students We have already used *Audubon*. It contains more information than the sections we have already used. Is this book fiction or nonfiction? *nonfiction*

Important to using different references is knowing how to find the information each book provides. Fortunately, nonfiction reference books list this type of information in a relatively uniform manner. Using the *Audubon* guide, look for these sections and note the following on table A.11:

---

1. Title Page:

   - Complete title: *National Audubon Society Field Guide to California*

   - Authors' names: *Peter Alden and Fred Heath*

   - Publisher and city: *Several publishers and cities are mentioned. Knopf, New York*

   - Year published: *2016*

2. Table of Contents:

   - How many parts? *3*

   - Names of parts: *Overview, Flora and Fauna, Parks and Preserves*

   - Your favorite section (sections are in bold): *Answers will vary.*

   - If you wanted to find out more about mushrooms, what page would you turn to? *page 82*

3. Index:

   - What page does this start on? *page 434*

   - How is it organized? *alphabetically*

   - If I wanted to find out more about Lake Tahoe, what pages could I turn to? *pages 12, 21, 421*

   - Find an animal, bird, or state/national park you like. What pages could you turn to find out more about it? *Answers will vary.*

---

4. Acknowledgements:

- What page does this section start on? Hint: use the Table of Contents. *page 429*

- What type of information do you learn about the authors in this section? *other authors who wrote sections; organizations that assisted the authors*

- Name a group or institution that helped the authors with their research. *Answers will vary.*

- Why should a reader review this section? *It gives the reader more information about how the book was written.*

5.1.2 History: Age of Exploration & Expedition

Teacher's Note In this section, your students will slowly move from looking at prehistory to the Spanish influence in California.

Big Question: How and why do people explore? (Murdoch, 2015)

Read to Students:

"...For the explorers saw some large marshes of a certain substance like pitch; they were boiling and bubbling, and the pitch came out mixed with an abundance of water. They noticed that the water runs to one side and the pitch to the other, and that there is such an abundance of it that it would serve to caulk many ships."

Source: Herbert Eugene Bolton, *Fray Juan Crespí: Missionary Explorer of the Pacific Coast 1769-1774* (Berkeley: University of California Press, 1927), 148-149.

- Do the "large marshes ... of pitch" remind you of anything? *tar pits*

- Where in California might these explorers be? *La Brea Tar Pits*

- From the stories you have heard so far, who else has used pitch? *Karana from Island of the Blue Dolphins*

Setting the Stage

Teacher's Note This section refers to 5 maps from Appendix B: figures B.4, B.5, B.6, B.7, and B.8. Ask your students to have these handy as you read the following history. Students should have colored markers available.

For a delightful reference that fills out the early folklore about Queen Calafia as well as stories about early explorers, check out *California, the Magic Island* by Doug Hansen. (Also listed in Suggestions for Younger Siblings.)

Big **Question**: Why is history worth knowing? (Murdoch, 2015)

Read to Students This passage about pitch marshes was written by Friar Juan Crespí on August 3, 1769. He was traveling on an expedition from Mexico to California with 2 now famous Spaniards – soldier and administrator Gaspar de Portolà and the Catholic Padre (Father) Junípero Serra. Their trip was known as the Sacred Expedition, and they were planning to build Catholic missions much like the ones they had already built in Mexico. They undertook this voyage from 1769-1782.

Review What type of a source is this Crespí passage? Primary or secondary? Fiction or Nonfiction? *primary, nonfiction*

Read to Students At the time of this expedition, Spain ruled parts of the United States, Mexico, Central America, and much of South America. Traveling from western Mexico, Juan Rodríguez Cabrillo, in the service of Spain, landed in San Diego in 1542 in search of a mythical all-water route through North America. Look at the map of Spain's Land Holdings in the Americas in the 1700s (figure B.4). On this map, Spain controlled all of the dark regions. Outline these darker regions with a colored marker.

Bonus If already covered, have students label regions of North, Central, and South America on figure B.4. See key for the regions of the Americas on figure C.2. If not already introduced, these regions will be covered in a later section.

Read to Students   Look at the Northern New Spain Map (figure B.5). What we now know as California was a region called New Spain; it was divided into Vieja California ("old," also known as Baja (lower) California), and Nueva (new) or Alta (upper) California. Shade in the areas of Nueva California and Vieja California, choosing a different color of marker for each area. [Note: The terms Nueva and Vieja are associated with Spanish rule/New Spain. Alta/Baja eventually were more commonly used and these names became the legal names when the region later fell under Mexican rule in 1824. (Source: Hubert Howe Bancroft, *History of California* (1884) page 68.)]

Father Junípero Serra and Gaspar de Portolà were part of an overland group which began in Loreto, Mexico, and entered Nueva California on foot, through San Diego. Looking at the Sacred Expedition Map (figure B.6), using a colored marker trace the line from Loreto, Mexico to San Diego.

Read   "A-Birding on a Bronco," in *California Out of the Box Supplement*, page 1 [*Stories from Where We Live*, page 187] to get an idea of what San Diego is like.

Discussion   The author is riding in San Diego county. What type of habitats does the author find herself in? *She mentions the chaparral, but the areas with grass and oaks are oak woodlands.*

Read to Students   The Spanish explorer Sebestián Vizcaíno had sailed previously to Monterey Bay in the early 17th century. He spoke of it as a deep harbor that could keep ships safe. Keeping Vizcaíno's travels in mind, the goal of the Sacred Expedition was to go as far north as this important bay in Monterey to build missions. But – Vizcaíno had seen Monterey Bay from the water. As the Spanish were walking overland, they ended up getting lost, not recognizing the bay from land. They went past Monterey to go as far north as San Francisco.

- Look at Google Earth with a satellite filter map to locate the cities of San Diego, Santa Barbara, Monterey, and San Francisco. **Google search terms: california map**

- Start in Santa Barbara, and look north along the coast. Trace the coast up to Monterey, and then to San Francisco.

- Using the Google Earth satellite map, what colors or landforms do you see on the coast between Santa Barbara and Monterey? Can you imagine why the Sacred Expedition didn't see Monterey Bay? *There is a lot of green – mountains – close to the coast. Depending on what trail in the mountains the Padres took, it's understandable that they wouldn't see the bay.*

Read the *Valley of the Moon*, "Historical Note," pages 200-201 (ending with "land grants").

Discussion Have students look at their Map of the Missions (figure B.7) and notice the missions.

1. How many missions are there? *21*

2. Which is the most southern? *San Diego de Alcalá*

3. Which is the farthest northward? *San Francisco Solano*

4. Which one was created first? *San Diego de Alcalá*

5. Which was built last? *San Francisco Solano*

6. Using Google, locate the 4 presidios. Add them to your Missions Map (figure B.7). **Google search terms: california presidios map**
   San Diego, Monterey, San Francisco, and Santa Barbara

Approximate locations key:

7. From your reading of the Historical Note in *Valley of the Moon*, how were the presidios different from the missions? *The presidios were built as forts for Spanish soldiers and their families.*

8. Why were the pueblos established? *They were small towns established for Spanish settlers who received land grants.*

9. Using Google again, find and locate the 2 pueblos. Mark them on your Missions Map (figure B.7). Google search terms: california pueblos on map *San Jose and Los Angeles*

Have students turn to their Map of the San Francisco Area (figure B.8). Using Google Maps, have students locate and number:

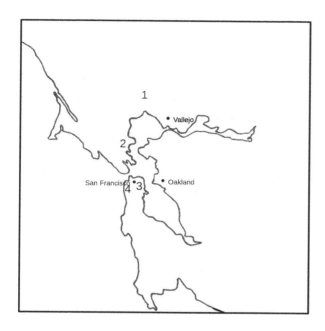

1. Mission Solano (Sonoma Mission)

2. Mission San Rafael

3. Mission San Francisco de Asís "Dolores"

4. San Francisco Presidio

Add to Timeline

- Years of the Sacred Expedition *1769-1782*

- Date and location of first mission *San Diego de Alcalá, 1769*

- Date and location of last mission *San Francisco Solano, 1823*

5.2   Week 9

Teacher's Note   As your students work through this next book, *Valley of the Moon*, they should listen carefully for how the main character, María Rosalia, describes her family background and ethnic traditions.

Instead of merely plot or sequence comprehension questions, students will be asked to recount how Maria Rosalia and her household celebrate festivals such as *Las Posadas* and *Día de los Muertos*.

Read to Students   Now we will go to the area of San Francisco, with its 3 missions and presidio. Pay attention to the main character, María Rosalia, and her family background and traditions.

5.2.1   Read *Valley of the Moon*, Pages 1-20

Big Question: Does the past make us who we are? (Murdoch, 2015)

1. How old was María Rosalia when she and her brother Domingo were found orphaned? *She was 5 and her brother was 2.*

2. What Native American tribe is Rosalia from? *Suisun tribe*

3. What is the story of how she came to live with the Medina family? *She was found by Padre Ygnacio at Mission San Rafael when she was 5, right after her mom died of small pox. When she was 9, the cook Lupita found her and brought her to live at the Medina rancho.*

4. How does Rosalia describe a *rancho*? *Vallejo had the grand rancho in Petaluma. Theirs is a copy – with balconies of rambling roses continually being added on. The walls are made of thick adobe. The family sleeps upstairs, and servants downstairs. The property is large, with crops such as herbs, beans, pumpkins, corn, and melons, and animals such as cattle, horses, pigs, and goats.*

5. How did she learn to read and write, and why might she need to conceal that she can? *She learned from Padre Ygnacio when he taught the mission boys to read. She needed to help Domingo, and in the process she too learned to read. She might need to conceal the fact that she can read and write because she is a female servant.*

5.2.2 Social Studies: Ethnicity

Teacher's Note The following paragraph begins the discussion of an important issue that is interwoven throughout the rest of the curriculum – the wonderful variety of ethnicities that exist in California.

Big Question: Can we belong to more than one culture? (Murdoch, 2015)

Read to Students Ethnicity is the cultural background of a person based on the fact that his or her their parents lived or were born in a certain area, or due to the traditions that the person learned (and continue) from his or her parents. People who live in a similar area tend to behave similarly. The weather, foods, and types of shelter are generally more alike if people reside in the same area.

How does Rosalia describe her ethnicity? What different cultures were her mother and father?

She is a self-described mestizo – half-Indian and half-white. Her skin is light in color. Her mother was Suisun Indian, and her dad may have been Spanish, a Russian fur trapper, or an American sailor.

5.2.3 History: Sutter's Fort

In pages 1-20, Johann Sutter is encouraging *americano* settlers to come to California.

Big Question: What motivates people to make long, dangerous journeys?

1. Where are the settlers/farmers coming from? *Missouri*

2. What major challenge do the settlers face in their journey? *They must travel through the snow-packed Sierra Nevadas.*

3. Sutter's Fort is an important place, with many goods and services being exchanged. Describe what it looks like and what types of businesses were there. *The walls were made of thick adobe, and due to the need to defend the fort, there were few windows. There were many businesses such as fur trade, weaving, carpentry, and blacksmithing.*

4. Find Sutter's Fort on Google Earth. Zoom out to locate the 2 major rivers nearby. Google search terms: sutters fort map

5. What 2 rivers converge near Sutter's Fort? *American and Sacramento Rivers.*

6. Video: Look at

   https://blogs.chapman.edu/huell-howser-archives/
   2002/08/12/sutters-fort-huell-howser/

   to see a half-hour video on the fort by Huell Hauser

7. What is the official name of the fort? What is Sutter's ethnic make-up? *The fort is named New Helvetia, which means New Switzerland. He was Swiss.*

8. Read the "Historical Note" in *Valley of the Moon* and finish page 201 to page 204 (through "former sailors").

9. According to the "Historical Note," what country controls California after 1821? *Mexico, not Spain anymore*

10. Use Google Maps to find Sonoma. Google search terms: sonoma california map

11. Add Sonoma to your California Map (figure B.2). See figure C.1 for key.

Review While heading to Sutter's Fort, Rosalia and Señor Johnston ride through what type of habitat? *oak woodlands*

Add to Timeline

- Date Spain accepts Mexican independence *1821*

- Year the missions closed (secularization) *1834*

5.2.4 Pages 20-38

. **Big Question**: What do people believe and why? (Murdoch, 2015)

1. Rosalia describes the day of rememberance *Día de los Muertos*. What do families observe in this tradition? *They remember family members who have passed away.*

2. Have students make a list of their family traditions. They can be religious in nature, or not. They should think about things they do together, repeatedly each year at the same time. It could be an outing or holiday, or even a special meal. If it is difficult to remember, have students look at pictures. *Examples include: Christmas and New Year celebrations, birthday parties, get togethers with grandparents, traditions at the beginning of the school year, yearly vacation trips, special meals.*

3. Rosalia goes to Mission San Rafael. What condition does she she find the mission in? *She finds the mission in shambles. There was a bird's nest in the chimney in the room where she grew up.*

4. Spend some time looking at Google Images of some photos of the missions (Google search terms: california missions photos). How would you describe what you see? What are some common elements you see about them? Look at the colors, materials, structure, shapes, and architecture.

They have domes, bells, crosses, thick walls; they are tall, white or off-white; they have lots of arches and red tiled roofs.

5. Which mission do you like the best?

5.2.5   Going Deeper into Family Traditions: *Día de los Muertos*

Big Question: How are religions the same and different? (Murdoch, 2015)

Read   *A Gift for Abuelita.* For book information see page 52. If resource is not available, another picture book about *Día de los Muertos* can be substituted.

1. What are some things Rosita did together with her Abuelita? *braiding, making tortillas, making salsa*

2. What are some items the family makes for their altar? *a lizard, flowers, a blanket, chicken in mole, and a braid*

3. What are some items they buy when they are in town for their altar? *candles, incense, apples and bread of the dead*

4. Which family members are they remembering? *Grandmother-Abuelita, Uncle-Tío, Grandfather-Abuelo, and Aunt-Tía*

5. What does the family do together at the grave? *They pull weeds and wash the gravestones. They set up a picnic.*

6. After Rosita has created the braid, how does she feel towards the end of the celebration? Is she satisfied? *By the end of the celebration, she feels her grandmother's closeness.*

7. Why do you think she chooses to make a braid? *Making braids was a special activity she did with her grandmother.*

8. Read the Author's Note.

5.2.6 Symbolism & Remembering Our Loved Ones

Teacher's Note The following section is included to aid families that don't have ancestor rememberance rituals to better understand the concept. If your students have a good understanding of such rituals, you may move on to Week 10.

Big Question: How do symbols communicate meaning? (Murdoch, 2015)

Research Have students use Google Images to briefly look at some *Día de los Muertos* altars. Google search terms: dia de los muertos altars

Discuss What are some materials you notice? What items do you see people including with their altars? *marigolds, photos, toys, skeletons, candles, food, skulls, fabric, and fruit*

Which altars do you like?

Written Reflection Have students spend some time remembering family members, or other loved ones or pets that have passed away. It may be helpful to make a list of people. Then have students each choose one family member to write a brief paragraph about. They should write about that person or their relationship. They can make the list and write this reflection in their Composition Book. Read the following questions to aid students in their reflections:

- Which person or pet who has died do you feel most connected with, and/or saddest about, and why?

- What was the person like?

- What do you miss the most about that person?

Sample paragraph: I miss my Grandma W. the most. She had a lot of very interesting hobbies that she taught me about. One of my favorites was when I was in the second grade, and she taught me how to make woven bead rings. She took me to the bead store to pick out my beads and then she spent the time to teach me how to do it.

Symbolism: Taking It Further   What is symbolism? Look up **symbolism** in dictionary. Think of a few examples.

Symbolism is using an object or word to express an abstract idea. Examples include: yin/yang, stop sign, school crossing sign, American flag, and the cross.

Visual Reflection   Rosita makes a braid for the altar to honor her grandmother's memory. What are some ways that you can visually or symbolically remember the family member you wrote about? *Students can draw a picture of person, go to places they liked, or keep a special momento of that family member.*

Have students draw a picture or create a model of an image that symbolizes their relationship or something they received from the deceased person or pet. It could be an image of places they went or something they learned from that person – even a memorable aspect of how that person dressed.

Sample idea: From my Grandma W, I would draw a graphic novel plate (sheet with 5 boxes) about the process of her teaching me how to make those rings. This set of images would be symbolic of my memory of her.

More information related to *Día de Los Muertos*:

Video: *How to Make Sugar Skulls for Day of the Dead* by MomsLA.

> https://www.youtube.com/watch?v=Rt146BqVMCg

5.3 Week 10

5.3.1 Pages 39-59

Big Question: Are we more the same or different from others? (Murdoch, 2015)

Lupita, Gregorio, and the Medinas are identied as **californios**.

1. What ethnicities are included in this cultural designation? *They were Spanish immigrants who settled in California during Spanish and Mexican rule. They are not caucasian.*

2. What language did they speak? *Spanish*

3. What was their predominant religion? *Catholicism*

4. What types of foods did they eat and how did they dress? *They ate Spanish foods and dressed in wealthy Spanish clothes.*

5. What 2-3 countries are they connected with? *Spain, Mexico, and Native Americans who were a part of the mission system. Native Americans (Indians) who did not learn Spanish in the missions are not considered californios.*

5.3.2   Religion: Our Lady of Guadalupe

Read to Students   Rosalia sees the Suisun Indians, led by Chief Solano, going to the Sonoma Mission for the Fiesta of the Virgin Guadalupe.

- How does Rosalia describe Guadalupe? *She is dark skinned, like the Indian people.*

- Use Google Images to find some pictures of Our Lady of Guadalupe. Google search terms: virgin Guadalupe images

- What other designs or symbols do you notice around the Virgin? *She is depicted standing with light radiating behind her, standing on a moon, with an angel below. Sometimes she is shown with roses on Diego's cloak.*

- Optional: sketch the figure of Our Lady of Guadalupe in your Sketch Book.

- Look for her image around where you live.

Bonus Where else besides California might people esteem her? *Mexico*

Reflection Imagine if you were from a Native American background. Would it be empowering for you to have a religious figure shown in your ethnicity? Why or why not?

5.3.3 Religious Traditions: *Las Posadas*

Big Question: What is a tradition, and why do we have them?

Discuss Rosalia celebrates *Las Posadas*.

- How does she describe this tradition?
  This holiday features a reenactment of the journey of Mary and Joseph seeking a place for Mary to have baby Jesus. Family and community members form a street procession, and are assigned different roles such as Mary, Joseph, and the angel. Participants are divided into two groups. While walking down the street, one group sings a verse to ask if there is room for Mary and Joseph, and the other group responds with a verse that there is no room. They do this several times until they knock at the last door and they are welcomed in. They have a party with bread and hot chocolate. During the evening they have religious plays about Bible stories, and finally a piñata. This procession is reenacted for 8 days prior to Christmas Eve.

- Have students write a brief paragraph describing how *Las Posadas* is celebrated. *They should include the information above.*

- How does your family celebrate Christmas, or any other winter holiday? *Answers will vary.*

- Optional: Read *Pedro: The Angel of Olvera Street* by Leo Politi (for book information see page 52). Where does this story take place? *Olvera Street, Los Angeles*

- The piñata is an important part of *Las Posadas*, and it is important in Latin American culture as well. You probably have hit one at a party too. Was it homemade or store bought?

- Watch this video:

  How to Make a Piñata by BeforeAndAfterTv.

  `https://www.youtube.com/watch?v=44JYARhkFe8`.

- As you watch this brief video, make a list of the necessary materials. How are piñatas made? What is the basic process? *Materials include: newspaper, crepe paper, scissors, glue, flour, water, balloon, party hats, paint brushes, string, and candy. The basic process is to blow up a balloon and cover it with newspaper papier-mâché. Five hats are taped on a balloon in a star formation. Colorful crepe paper is added, and the piñata is finally stuffed with candy.*

- If time permits, make one!

5.3.4   Pages 60-80

Big Question: Why can one problem be solved multiple ways?

1. What 2 different ways does the Medina family try to cure Rafaella's sickness? *The white doctors give her medicines. Lupita, who has Native American ancestry, goes to her people to obtain curative roots and herbs.*

2. On pages 79-80, the Medina family rides to Sonoma for *Candlemas*. What is celebrated on this day, and how? *This is the festival of of the day Jesus was dedicated in the temple, 40 days after he was born. They have a parade and a blessing of the candles. After mass doves are released.*

3. Mariano Vallejo's German brother-in-law, Jacob Leese, celebrates Groundhog's Day on February 2. What does this holiday celebrate? *It is believed that if a groundhog pops up and sees his shadow, he will get scared and run back in his hole; winter will be 6 weeks longer. If it is a cloudy day when he pops up, he will not be scared of his shadow and the winter will be mild.*

5.4 Week 11

5.4.1 History: California Missions

Teacher's Note In this section, students will do a brief research project on a mission of their choice. Online research resources are provided on the next page.

For a good library resource, check out *The California Missions Source Book : Key Information, Dramatic Images, and Fascinating Anecdotes Covering All 21 Missions* by author David J. McLaughlin (ISBN: 9781937313005). Alternatively, a copy of information contained in this book can also be found at the www.missionscalifornia.com website listed below.

Big Question: Where is the past in the present? (Murdoch, 2015)

Read to Students Lupita, Gregorio, Ramona, and Rosalia have all lived a part of their lives at a mission. You have looked at pictures of some of the missions. Begin to research one of the missions. Using the Mission Research Chart (table A.12), write one to three paragraphs in your Composition Books and include the following:

1. Name and location of the mission

2. What is its informal name, if any?

3. When was it built? Who founded it?

4. Who is the patron saint?

5. Draw the floor plan.

6. Who built it?

7. What tribe(s) lived there?

8. How were families housed in the mission?

9. What did children do there?

10. How many converts (*neophytes*) were there?

11. Does the mission have any notable industries?

12. Other interesting facts?

13. Include a photo of the mission.

Reflection   Imagine how a child who is Native American might live differently after spending time at a mission? After only knowing the mission, would he or she be able to go back and live with their tribe?

Resources   In addition to your local library, here are some good online resources:

Good overview (California Missions Resource Center):
`http://www.californias-missions.org/`

Resources on each mission:
`http://www.missionscalifornia.com/index.html`

5.4.2   Pages 81-110

Teacher's Note   The following table, table A.13, asks students to classify characters as *californio* or not. The distinguishing aspect to this designation is that the person speaks Spanish, and the more Castillan the Spanish, the more *californio* they are. Native Americans in California like Rosalia who are Catholic, speak Spanish, live at a mission, and relate with Mexicans/Spaniards (more than their Native tribe) can also be considered *californio*. This curriculum uses a wide interpretation of this designation.

Big Question: Does our language impact who we relate with?

1. Read "Historical Note" from 204-205 (to "bloody battles began").

2. Finish Missions Project.

3. In these pages, what country controls California? What group seems to be moving in? *Mexico controls California. The US seems to be moving in.*

4. Name some of the *californios* in this section. *Sr. Medina, General Vallejo*

5. Who would not be considered a *californio*? *Henry, Walter, and Nelly Johnston*

Read to Students Fill in the *Californio* Table (table A.13) and put an "x" in the correct box. If the person doesn't fit into either, just label "neither."

Character	*californio*	*americano*
Señor Medina	x	
Captain Frémont		x
Señor Villareal	x	
Henry Johnston		x
Johann Sutter		x
Gregorio	x	
Lupita	x	
Rosalia	x	
Walter Johnston		x
Mariano Vallejo	x	
Domingo	x	
Nelly Johnston		x
Padre Ygnacio	x	
Miguela	x	

5.4.3 Drawing Comparisons: Venn Diagrams

Big Question: Are we more the same or more different from others? (Murdoch, 2015)

Read to Students   Karana lived on San Nicolas Island by herself until she was about 30 years old. Rosalia lived with her mom until her mom died when she was 5, and then she lived as an orphan at Mission San Rafael for about 4 years, when she was found by Gregorio and Lupita and taken to the Medina *rancho*. What are some ways Rosalia's experiences are similar to and/or different from the character of Karana?

To illustrate your reflections, you will use a **Venn diagram**. This type of diagram helps to illustrate how things are similar and different. For qualities that only have to do with Karana, place in the circle with Karana's name. The same is true for Rosalia. For events or qualities that are true of both, place them in the overlapping part of the circles. In your reflections, consider lifestyle, transportation, shelter, mission involvement, family, religion, geography, and food.

Review and Reflect   Fill in the Karana vs. Rosalia Venn Diagram (figure B.9.) See key on the following page for possible answers.

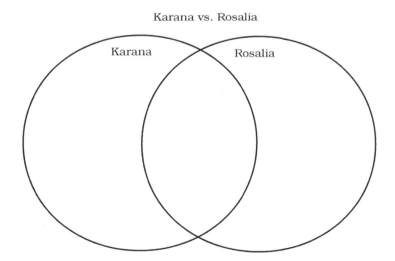

Karana	Both	Rosalia
Knows how to live off the land		Dependent on Medina family
	Both ended up at missions	
	Both lived with brothers for at least part of the story	
Lived in the way of Native tribe		Is not connected to the ways of her mother's tribe
	Both do not live with birth mom or dad during much of the story	
	Both are female	
Hunts and harvests		Harvests crops
Not many formal religious traditions		Lots of religious traditions
Walks everywhere		Rides in horsedrawn carriages
Uses fire for light, cooking, and warmth		Uses candles for light
Lives alone for most of story		Lives with Medina family
Nicoleño tribe		Half Suisun Native American
	Both alive in 1845	
Lived in Santa Barbara area		Lived in the San Francisco Bay area
Based on a real person		Character of historical fiction

5.4.4   Immigration Stories: How We Came

Teacher's Note   After reflecting on the differences between Karana and Rosalia, your students will begin the How We Came Tracker. This chart will map various journeys to California. As your students continue in this curriculum, they will add to this chart.

Big Question: Does where we come from matter?

Read to Students   As you read this book, notice the ways characters have come to California. In *Valley of the Moon* and *Island of the Blue Dolphins*, there are people of different ethnicities who settle in California. Locate your How We Came Tracker (table A.14), and fill it in for the following characters/people in the last 2 books:

- Karana

- Junípero Serra & overland Sacred Expedition (students may need to look up where Serra was born)

- María Rosalia

- Walter & Nelly Johnston

See figure C.3 for How We Came Tracker Key.

5.4.5   Pages 110-130

Big Question: Why do we watch animal races?

1. Describe the cockfight that Señor Medina attends with Domingo. How does Rosalia describe the event? Using Google Images, look for some pictures of a cockfight. Draw a picture of what you imagine Paladín looks like. **Google search terms: cockfight rooster images** *Only men go to the cockfight. They keep the cocks in cages, and they have special spurs for them.*

2. What are the *herraderos*? If you were there, what would you see, and how would it be set up?

   The herraderos is the rounding up and branding of young cattle. There are also other competitions such as riding unbroken horses and knocking cows off balance. There is a platform for the musicians and bleachers; the ladies sit on one side, and the men sit on the other, all in their finest dress. Indians sat outside and traded with the californios.

5.4.6 State Symbol: The Grizzly Bear

Brief Research   A grizzly bear takes some of the Medinas berries. Have students look up some pictures in Google Images of a close cousin of the California Grizzly Bear - the North American Grizzly Bear. Google search terms: north american grizzly bear photos

Read more about the California Grizzly Bear at the following link, under "State Animal."

`http://www.library.ca.gov/history/symbols.html`

5.5   Week 12

5.5.1   Pages 130-150

Big Question: Who should rule, and why? (Murdoch, 2015)

1. General Castro is assembling resources to mount a defense against the *americanos*. What is his plan (that might provoke the *americanos*)? *He and his men are gathering horses; they will ride out from Monterey to Vallejo's house in Sonoma to chase the Americans out.*

2. While the family is in Sonoma, a significant event occurs, the **Bear Flag Revolt**. What happens in this event on June 14, 1846? Who has revolted? Who was arrested? What is the ethnic make-up of the *osos*? *A group of Americans dressed as fur trappers attacked Castro's men (the californios), and told Castro's men not to attack white settlers.*

The white Americanos are "osos" (or bears). They arrest Vallejo. They make a flag with a red star and a grizzly bear, and call themselves the California Republic. They take the Mexican flag down in Sonoma and put theirs up. William B. Ide is their leader.

3. Using Google Images, find a picture of the Bear Flag. In your Sketch Book, draw a picture of the flag. Google search terms: bear flag revolt flag photo

Source: Starscream, "Bear Flag Revolt," *Wikimedia Commons*, accessed July 9, 2018, https://commons.wikimedia.org/wiki/File:Original_Todd_bear_flag.jpg, public domain.

5.5.2   Pages 151-160

Big Question: What happens when cultures collide?

1. Finish "Historical Note," pages 205-208.

2. What happens on July 7, 1846? What towns do the Americans begin take? How long has the Republic of California lasted? *On July 7, 1846, the US flag is raised in Monterey. The Americans take Monterey, Yerba Buena, and Sonoma. The Republic of California has lasted 21 days.*

3. What happened to California after the 1847 peace agreement with Mexico and the Treaty of Guadalupe Hidalgo? *California and a few other states such as Nevada, New Mexico, and Arizona were sold by Mexico to the United States.*

4. What government controlled California beginning in 1848? *the United States*

5. When Rosalia looks down on her small pox scar, what mystery does this provoke? *She wonders who her father is.*

Add to Timeline

- Date of Bear Flag Revolt *June 14, 1846*

- Year Mexico lost California *1848* (You may need to look up the exact year of the Treaty of Guadalupe Hidalgo)

- Year California became a state *1850*

  Important: Pause & Review

- From 1847-1851, what major ownership change happens in California? *In 1847, Mexico controls California. By 1850, California is a US state.*

- If Mexico had known gold was discovered, do you think they would have sold their land to the US?

5.5.3 Pages 160-180

Big Question: Why do people take sides in conflicts?

1. When Gregorio and Rosalia are headed to Yerba Buena to find Padre Ygnacio at Mission Rafael, they see many Mexicans in transit. Where are some places the Mexicans are fleeing to now that Alta California is a part of the United States? *Mexicans are headed back to Mexico and more remote ranchos in California.*

2. Where does Rosalia hear Fremont and the *Osos* are going next, after successfully planting the US flag in many northern California cities? What does the US expect to find in the south? *She hears they are*

headed to the south, to cities such as Los Angeles. The "Osos" expect to find more resistance to US rule there.

Bonus   Why might Vallejo burn his Mexican uniform when he gets released from Sutter's Fort? *Vallejo acknowledged that Mexican rule was over, and he thought that California would be better off under American rule. He wanted to encourage californios to accept US rule.*

Reflection   Rosalia hears Walter is glad that the Americans have "rescued" California from the Spanish. Why might she be sad about this comment? Why might Walter be glad California is "rescued?" *Rosalia might be sad because she identifies with the Spanish, Mexicans, and californios. Walter might be glad because he identifies with the Americans.*

5.6   Week 13

5.6.1   Pages 180-188

Big Question: Does the past make us who we are? (Murdoch, 2015)

1. Who does Rosalia find out her mother was? *Her mother was the daughter of a shaman from a Native tribe; she was in the process of learning about roots and herbs.*

2. Who was Rosalia's father, and what was his ethnic background? Where did he work? *Her father, Antonio Medina, was of criollos/Spanish background and worked at the presidio.*

3. How did the father image in her dreams connect with real life? *He was the man with the moustache from the hallway painting.*

4. What type of a person was her mother? *Her mother was a giving and self-sacrificing person. She gave her own doses of smallpox vaccine to her children.*

5. How has Rosalia's standing changed now that she finds out her father, Señor Medina's brother, had a rancho in the Sacramento Valley? *It has*

improved. She changes her last name to Medina and gets access to her father's wealth.

6. What is the last thing she does at Mission San Rafael for her mother? *She makes a new headstone for her mom.*

5.6.2 Epilogue

.

Read the Epilogue.

1. What are the 2 driving forces of much of the change at the *rancho* properties in the late 1840s and 50s? How do the *rancho* owners fare? *The discovery of gold and California statehood caused much change on the ranchos. The rancho owners do not fare well, as they must prove they own land to the US government, which makes many people penniless, such as Señor Medina.*

2. How does Henry Johnston make money during the Gold Rush? *He makes money selling goods to miners.*

3. How do you think Rosalia turns out after this diary? How does she start and end? Does her life and ending surprise you? *Yes. She goes from being an orphan servant girl to owning land and starting a winery.*

5.6.3   Reflection: *Antiguo*
Major Changes in California in the 1800s

Big Questions: How do living things change as they grow? (Murdoch, 2015)

Teacher's Note In this section your students will briefly review life under Native, Spanish, and then American influence. There was tremendous change during this period technology wise – from handmade spears to guns and firepower. Your students should understand this change in a broad way. Don't be concerned if they cannot recount exact specifics. Help them remember the stories. Answer these questions, and fill in the answers on the Part I Review (table A.15).

Discussion:

1. Remembering back to *Island of the Blue Dolphins*, how did Karana live? How did she make her home? How did she make her tools? What did she eat, and how did she kill/find her food?
   She lives off the land. She makes her home from whale bones and kelp. She makes her tools from sticks and seal tusks. She eats roots, shellfish, and fish. She kills her food with a spear and harvests shellfish.

2. As you move to the time of the missions and the *ranchos*, how did the Medinas build their home? What materials did they use? How did they make their tools? What foods did they eat? How did they find their foods, and what did they use to hunt with? How did the Medina family obtain goods such as fabrics, sugar, flour, and tools that they did not make themselves?
   The Medinas built their structure much like ours today, but with wood and adobe. They made their tools by blacksmithing and trading. They ate foods they grew on their property: meats from their animals, vegetables and fruits. They also went hunting with guns. Items they did not make or grow they got from trading centers such as Henry Johnston's store or Sutter's Fort.

Reflection Table Have students fill in the following chart (table A.15) with their reflections. Have students add a category of their choice to compare. See completed chart below.

Item	Karana	Rosalia
Homes	*Whale-bone wood and kelp house, sleeping rock, cave hideouts*	*Rancho building with balconies with rambling roses, made of wood and adobe*
Tools	*Spears, bull kelp net, canoe*	*Guns, wagons, pen and ink*
Foods	*Abalone and other shellfish, fish, roots, eggs*	*Tamales, tortillas, various meats, hot chocolate, candies, pan de muerto*
Other (Ideas: clothing, transportation, religion, daily jobs)		

3. **Bonus:** Though Rosalia and Karana lived at about the same time, their lives were very different. What are some of the biggest differences between them? Hint: think about disease, living alone, land ownership, their fathers' ethnicities, geography.
   Karana lived alone; Rosalia did not. Karana had to work with resources on hand; Rosalia had access to traded goods. Rosalia had immunity to smallpox and white man's diseases; Karana did not and may have died from one of these diseases. Rosalia became a wealthy landowner; Karana did not have a formalized claim to her island. Rosalia had a Spanish dad; Karana was 100% native. Karana lived on a remote island; Rosalia lived in the heavily settled area of Sonoma/San Francisco Bay area.

4. **Reflection:** Moving from a Native American experience to the *rancho* period: What force(s) do you think brought about the modernization that can be seen in Rosalia's life? Consider colonialism, US politics, and discoveries.
   The fall of the missions, California statehood (1850), and the discovery

of gold impacted Rosalia's life more, as she lived in the San Francisco Bay area, which was closer to the action. Her lifestyle was more impacted by immigrants coming to the new state – she had access to new foods, tools, and more advanced construction techniques.

5.7   Week 14

5.7.1   Social Science: Native American Population, 1770-1970

Teacher's Note   In this section your students will take a closer look at the Native American population.

Big Question: Why do people groups grow or shrink?

Read to Students   What ethnicities have we talked about so far in our study of California? Let's make a list. *Native Americans, Spanish, white settlers, Mexicans, Russians, Aleuts*

1. Of these groups, which do you imagine are growing in the 1850s? *white settlers*

2. Which are shrinking during this time? *Mexican, Spanish, Native American, Russian, Aleut*

Data Project

Have students look at table A.16.

Population of Native Americans in California, 1770-1970

Year	Number of Native Americans in California (estimated and rounded to thousands)
1770	310,000
1830	245,000
1845	150,000
1855	50,000
1880	20,000
1900	15,000
1910	20,000
1933	22,000
1955	36,000
1960	39,000
1970	91,000

Source: Sherburne F. Cook, "Historical Demography," in *Handbook of North American Indians, Vol. 8: California*, ed. Robert F. Heizer (Washington, D.C.: Smithsonian Institution, 1978), 91-98.

Discussion Examine this table of the Population of Native Americans in California 1770-1970 (table A.16). We will look at the changes in population.

Population is the number of living beings of the same group or species which live in a particular geographical area, in this case, the state of California.

1. According to this table, when was the native population the highest? *1770*

2. When was the population the lowest? What year does it start to increase? *Native population is the lowest in 1900. It starts to increase in 1910.*

3. From the stories so far, what are some of the reasons you think the Native American population has decreased? Why might it start to increase? *It decreased due to contact with Spanish diseases and violent attacks*

against them. Also, the native people who had contact with the missions lost their traditions and way of life. They could not easily go back to their tribes after the mission system ended. Their population may have begun to increase as life became more stable in California, and there was greater rule of law.

Bonus: Chart Work   For more advanced students (5th-6th grade), you may choose to do the following exercise.

Big Question: What do graphs tell us? (Murdoch, 2015)

Read and Discuss   It is helpful to put numbers into a graphical format to see the patterns. One such graphical device is a chart. Charts have 2 axes – the X and Y axes. The X axis runs horizontally on the bottom, and the Y axis runs vertically. The corner where they meet is the origin. When making a chart, it is important to label the axis with the information you are showing on each axis. Also, charts are given a title.

Using the information in table A.16, fill in chart A.17:

- Label the X and Y axis

- Place a dot on the population number for the corresponding year.

- One by one, starting in 1770, connect the dots each year. Note: year increments correspond to exact year on chart.

- Title your chart

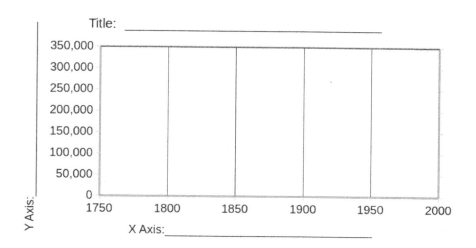

Title: _____

Y Axis: _____

X Axis: _____

Answer key:

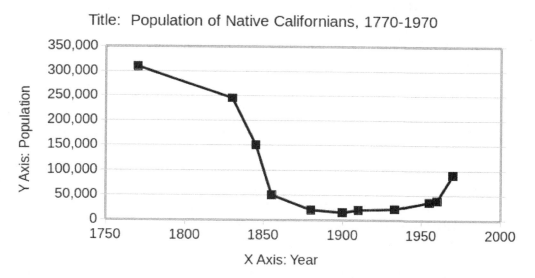

Title: Population of Native Californians, 1770-1970

Y Axis: Population

X Axis: Year

5.7.2 End of *Antiguo* Questions (Units I & II)

Questions for further consideration:

1. What big question do you have? What do you want to do about it?

2. Reflect on the title *Antiguo*. What does this word mean? Make a list of some of the former things in California, prehistory to 1845, considering – humans, animals, and history. Reflecting on your list, what three changes are the most significant to you, and why?
   Antiguo means ancient or former. Some of the former things include: pygmy mammoths, sabertooth tigers, missions, and ranchos. Some of the significant changes include: Pleistocene animals are gone, Native American population is much smaller, the missions have come and gone, and Spain and Mexico no longer rule California.

3. Imagine gold had been discovered before the Bear Flag Revolt in June of 1846. How do you think Mexico would have approached its remote territory of Alta California? *Mexico would not have been as willing to relinquish the land. The white settlers would have been even more forceful in taking the land.*

4. Why didn't Native Americans just go back to live on their tribal lands after the mission system ended? What ways did they change while at the missions? Think about the impact of the mission system on children, language, daily life, and religion.
   Many families were broken apart at the missions. Children lived separately from their parents. As a result, a generation of young kids missed out on learning their native culture. Families might have adapted to life in buildings and wearing clothes. They also learned Spanish and what it meant to be Catholic from the Padres.

5. If you could live in Karana's or Rosalia's place, which would you pick, and why?

6. Are the people in Nueva/Alta California very different from the people in Vieja/Baja California, then and now? What ways are the colonial influences similar? Why do you think the physical border between the US and Mexico sits where it does? (Hint: Look at the border on maps and notice surrounding states, etc.) *People in Alta and Baja*

California both were ruled by Spain and then Mexico. They shared a common Latin background. Now Alta California is more different, as we have people from all over the US and world who have come here. The border might sit where it does because the lower part of what we now know as California is just above the peninsula (Baja California).

7. In the end, was the mission system good for each of these characters: Rosalia, Domingo, Rosalia's Mom, Lupita, Señor Medina, Miguela? Why or why not? *The mission system was not good for Rosalia's mom, as she died of a disease. It was not good for Lupita or Señor Medina in the end because they lost the Medina rancho. The system was good for Rosalia, Domingo, and Miguela, as they were all able to retain their property when California became a state.*

8. In both books you have read so far, what are some factors that drew people to California? Why *did* people come (trappers, Mexicans, missionaries, people from central and eastern United States)? *White settlers came to California for land; the Spanish missionaries came to assert their ownership of Alta California and make Catholic converts; the fur trappers came to get wealth from otter pelts, and Mexicans came to get land grants after Spain no longer controlled California.*

Unit III

¡Oro!

(Gold)

The Great Rush for Gold

Chapter 6

Unit Introduction

6.1   Supplies for This Unit

1. Resources used throughout

   - See list on page 2

2. Chapter 7: *By the Great Horn Spoon!*

   - *By the Great Horn Spoon!* (Sid Fleischman, ISBN 978-0-316-28612-1)

   - Treasure map making supplies such as brown craft paper, Sharpies, markers, and pencils (see "Geography: Treasure Maps," page 96)

   - Russet potatoes (at least 3, the older the better)

   - Clippings of several hardy green plants

   - Various other materials students choose for the "Science: Water Potatoes?," page 97

   - Various materials depending on projects chosen for "History: A Miner's Life Activities," page 110

   - Optional Habitat Home Building Supplies. See "Habitat Study: Coast and Islands" (section 2.2.2, page 18) for project description.

Chapter 7

By the Great Horn Spoon!

7.1 Week 15

Read to Students And now, we take another journey to California – that of 12-year-old Jack Flagg and his butler Praiseworthy. To begin their story, you will go to the eastern seaboard of the United States to the city of Boston, Massachusetts.

As you read this story, pay careful attention to the places their seagoing journey takes them. Where does their ship stop along the way?

Also, pay attention to the way their lives change as they become gold miners. How do they live, dress, and adapt to their California adventure?

7.1.1 Chapters 1-2

Big Question: How and why do people move from place to place?

1. How have these stowaways gained passage aboard the *Lady Wilma*? *Jack and Praiseworthy gained passage by hiding in potato barrels because their money had been stolen.*

2. Why have they decided to make this journey? *Jack's parents passed away, so his Aunt Arabella took charge of him and his two younger sisters. Arabella suffered hard financial times, and Jack and Praiseworthy decided to make money on the goldfields to help her out.*

94

3. Where did they start their trip, and where are they headed? What will their route be? How long will it take them? *They started in Boston and will travel to California. They will go around Cape Horn; the journey should take them a few months.*

4. If they did not go around the Cape, how else could they get to California? How long would this journey take? *They could go overland, but this could take as long as 1 year.*

5. Find Map of the Americas, figure B.10 in Appendix B.

   - Using Google Earth, find and label the names of the 3 parts of the Americas: North, Central, and South America. **Google search terms: map of the americas**

   - Locate and label Boston, Massachusetts.

   - Locate and label Cape Horn.

   - Locate and label the state of California, putting a dot in San Francisco Bay.

   - Locate and label Mexico.

For key, see Map of the Americas Key, figure C.2 in Appendix C.

7.1.2 Chapters 3-4

Big Question: What can you learn from going to faraway places?

1. Where is Jack and Praiseworthy's first stop? *Rio*

2. Research: Using Google Maps, find Rio. Zoom out to find in which of the Americas, and in which country Rio is located. **Google seach terms: rio map** *Rio is located in South America, in Brazil.*

3. Locate and label Rio on your Map of the Americas, Figure B.10. Draw a route in the ocean connecting Boston and Rio. *For key, see Map of the Americas Key, figure C.2.*

4. Use Google Images to find some pictures of Rio. **Google search terms: rio city photos**

7.1.3   Geography: Treasure Maps

Big Question: What can we learn from looking at old maps?

One of Dr. Buckabee's most cherished possessions is his treasure map.

Use Google Images to view some pictures of treasure maps. Google search terms: ancient treasure map photos

For a beautiful source of old maps, visit:

`https://www.davidrumsey.com`

- Which are your favorite, and why?

- Draw a treasure map for a friend or member of your family to use to find some treasure you will hide. To make it look antique, use craft or brown paper. Have an adult lightly singe the edges.

7.2   Week 16

7.2.1   Chapters 5-6

Big Question: Do shortcuts pay off?

1. How does the *Lady Wilma* end up going around South America? Using Google Images, find, locate, and label this area on your Map of the Americas, figure B.10. Draw a route from Rio through the straits. Hint: students may need to look up a picture of this route through the straits. Google search terms: straits of magellan map
   The Lady Wilma goes around the Straits of Magellan. See figure C.2 for a key.

2. What route does the *Sea Raven* take? Was it a good choice for the *Lady Wilma* to go through the straits? *The Sea Raven goes around Cape Horn. Though stormy and dangerous, it was a good idea for the Lady Wilma to go through the straits as this choice saved time and fuel.*

3. Use Google Earth or Google Images to look at the land in the area of Tierra del Fuego and the Straits of Magellan. How would you describe the terrain? What weather and colors do you see on the land? **Google search terms: tierra del fuego straits of magellan photos**
   The area is green and snowy, with high mountains, unusual rock formations, and penguins.

4. At this point in the voyage, they are running low on what supplies? *water and coal*

5. The Frenchman has grape cuttings he is trying to keep alive, in spite of the shortages. How do they end up saving them? *They put the cuttings into Azariah Jones' rotting potatoes, as the potatoes are turning to water as they rot.*

7.2.2 Science: Water Potatoes?

Teacher's Note The following project is a free form science project. The challenge is for students to recreate the idea of getting water from a vegetable through trial and error. This may take some time, 1-2 months or more, especially if starting with new potatoes. On the *Lady Wilma* they had been traveling for at least 2 months before their potatoes went bad. Get a plate going where students can house their potatoes for a while. Remember, molds and growths are not all bad!

Big Question: Is it possible to get water from a plant?

Writing Have students write in their Composition Books **how** they will put their clippings in the potatoes. **What** do they think will happen? If it doesn't work, what **other ideas** do they have to keep their clippings alive inside a potato? What **conditions** help potatoes turn to water faster (e.g., temperature, moisture, light, time)? What do students notice **growing** on the potatoes as they turn to water?

After students set up their 1st potatoes, have students fill out Water Potato Observations, table A.18.

Project   Materials:

- 3 Potatoes (the older, the better)

- Clippings of green plants

- Various other materials for techniques students might use to get water out of a potato

1. Using one potato, cut a small hole or a slit, and insert a clipping of a live plant.

2. Fill out Water Potato Observations, table A.18.

3. How long does clipping stay alive?

4. If this experiment does not work, try other variations. Using the other two or more potatoes, what other ways can students keep a plant sprig alive?

5. Add other two potatoes to table A.18.

Attempt #	Start date	End date	How	Notes	Clipping Result

7.2.3 Chapters 7-8

Big Question: Have you been to an extreme location, in terms of altitude or temperature? What can you learn about life in extreme places?

1. What city and country does the *Lady Wilma* stop next? *Callao, Peru*

2. Using Google, locate and label Callao on Map of the Americas, figure B.10. Draw a route from the straits to this city. **Google search terms: callao map**

3. Look at some photos of Callao and the Andes mountains using Google Images. How would you describe what you see? **Google search terms: callao city photos and andes photos**
   Callao is a modern seaside city. The Andes are very tall, with snow and unique rock formations.

4. Describe Praiseworthy. What does a butler do? What type of family would hire him? How does he dress? *A butler helps a wealthy family with a large house or household. In a large estate, sometimes butlers have charge of all other waitstaff such as the maids and cooks. He wears a bowler hat and carries an umbrella.*

5. In these chapters, he loses his bowler hat overboard. What does he replace his hat with? *He replaces his hat with a handkerchief.*

6. The *Lady Wilma* stops at a group of islands off the coast of Ecuador called the Galápagos Islands. Using Google, locate, label, and draw a route from Callao to these islands on your Map of the Americas, figure B.10. **Google search terms: galapagos islands map** *See key at figure C.2.*

7. Use Google Maps to locate Mexico and San Francisco. Complete their sea journey on your Map of the Americas (figure B.10) by tracing their journey from the Galápagos Islands, passing Mexico, and arriving in San Francisco Bay. **Google search terms: map central and north america**

8. How many miles have they traveled? *15,000 miles*

9. In Chapter 8, they arrive in San Francisco and see lots of different ethnicities. What people groups do they see? *They see Islanders, East Indians, Chinese, Mexicans, and Chileans.*

10. How long has it taken for them to get to California? *5 months*

11. Add Jack and Praiseworthy (combined on 1 line) to your How We Came Tracker, table A.14.

12. Jack and Praiseworthy find they are short of money to get a hotel room plus the riverboat fare to Sacramento. What way do they come up with to make money? *They strike up a business cutting miners' hair.*

13. Quartz Jackson teaches them about panning for gold. What do they learn from him? How much per ounce is gold selling for? *Gold is heavy and sinks to the bottom of the pan. It is selling for $14 per ounce.*

7.2.4   Unique Habitat: The Galápagos Islands

Teacher's Note   In this section, students will briefly look into these unique islands that are unfortunately omitted from many studies. This section is intended to be a brief foray.

Big Question: How are different landmasses connected?

Source: Don Mammoser/Shutterstock.com, standard license.

Read to Students   The Galápagos Islands have some special features.

Using Google Images, look at some photos of the islands. Google search terms: galapagos island photos

1. What animals do you see? *turtles, lizards, birds*

2. Use these resources to explore what makes them unusual.

   Informative Overview Video (*Welcome to the Galapagos Islands* by oceancontent):

   https://www.youtube.com/watch?v=TzAvFtQv3oQ

   This Unesco World Heritage site is a good source of information; it also has short videos on the notable species:

   http://whc.unesco.org/en/list/1/.

   Bonus   This Cornell site has an excellent section on Galápagos geology:

   http://www.geo.cornell.edu/geology/Galapagos.html

Pre-Writing Discussion

1. What rare types of animals and plants are found? *flightless cormorants, land iguanas, marine iguanas, giant turtles, penguins, rare cacti*

2. How many islands are a part of this group? *19*

3. How would you describe the land and undersea habitat? *lava rock flows, volcanic cones, slight vegetation, rich undersea life, lava vents*

4. What famous biologist visited the island in 1835? *Charles Darwin*

5. How were these islands formed? *volcanic activity*

Writing Taping an index card in your Composition Book, draw a picture of the landscape or an animal found on the islands. Write a paragraph that includes information from the previous discussion.

Bonus Island Living: just as Karana adapted to live on San Nicolas Island by herself, how has the Galápagos marine iguana adapted to living on an island with low vegetation? Briefly research ways this iguana has adapted to harsh conditions. Review the section on Adaptations and Consequences found on page 16 if needed.

Each of the islands hosts a unique marine iguana, with different colors and shapes. They have white salt patches encrusted on their heads to help rid salt they accumulate while swimming. Their flatened tails and sharp nails and teeth help them swim and eat algae off rocks in the ocean. Their black color enables them to absorb heat while they are sun bathing after swimming in the frigid waters.

Bonus From the Cornell geology site, what three "plates" are closest to these islands? (These plates will be discussed in the next unit.) *South America Plate, Cocos Plate, and the Nazca Plate*

Review Finally, the *Lady Wilma* heads from these islands off Ecuador, past Mexico to the San Francisco Bay. Who else have you heard about who came to California through Mexico? *Juníperro Serra and the Sacred Expedition*

7.3   Week 17

7.3.1   Chapters 9-10

Big Question: When we go on a journey, in what ways can we tell our story to others?

1. How do Jack and Praiseworthy get to Sacramento City? Using Google Earth, locate the portion of the Sacramento River that goes from San Francisco Bay to Sacramento. Trace the outline of the river between these 2 cities on the your California Map, figure B.2. **Google search**

terms: sacramento river

They go by riverboat from SF to Sacramento. See figure C.1 for a California Map Key.

2. Which mining camp do they decide to go? How to they get there? How much money are they able to make when they sell their pick and shovel? *They go to Hangtown. They get there by stagecoach, using $100 from the sale of their pick and shovel.*

3. **Bonus** You have considered Native Americans in the characters of Karana and María Rosalia. In this story, the Native Americans are referred to as "Digger Indians." Look up this definition. Why might Jack be afraid to meet them? Are his fears warranted? **Google search terms: digger indian definition**

   Digger Indian is a derogatory term applied to Native peoples of the Great Basin, which came to be used to describe Indians in the areas of the mining camps. Jack is afraid they will attack him. Praiseworthy assures him they are harmless, and they were only are digging for roots and acorns.

4. Using the maps on the backflap of the *Audubon* guide, if you are Jack and Praiseworthy in Sacramento looking to the East, what mountain range would you see? *Sierra Nevadas*

5. In Chapter 10, Jack and Praiseworthy find out that Cut-Eye Higgins has gone through the Panama Canal to come to California. Using Google, locate the Panama Canal. On your Map of the Americas (figure B.10), locate the Panama Canal and label it. Using a different color marker or pencil (than the color you used for Jack and Praiseworthy), mark Cut-Eye Higgin's journey from Boston, through the Panama Canal, to San Francisco. **Google search terms: panama canal map** *See figure C.2 for a key.*

6. Add Cut-Eye Higgins to your How We Came Tracker, table A.14. Hint: you may need to look up how long the journey took coming California via the Panama isthmus. **Google search terms: panama canal journey gold rush**

   The journey took 2-3 months if taking the canal shortcut.

Reflection   How does the label in these chapters of "Digger Indians" contrast with what you have learned about Native Americans though other characters, such as Karana and Rosalia? Is it a flattering term? Why might a white boy see Native Americans in this way?

Jack is a person of privledge. Digger Indian is a derogatory (negative) term that stereotypes Native Americans. The Native Americans were defending their land against outsiders. In doing so, they attacked people of other ethnicities who were taking their land, which put fear in newcomers such as Jack.

Can you think of other racist or derogatory terms you've heard? *Answers will vary.*

7.3.2   History: CD Parkhurst

Read "The Secret of CD Parkhurst" in *The California Coast* reader (*Stories from Where We Live*), beginning on page 39.

Big Question: Why do people keep secrets?

1. What are some of the dangers that Charlie faced as a stagecoach driver? *bandits, breaking bridges, runaway horses, cold damp weather*

2. What discovery was made after Charlie died? *Charlie was a woman!*

3. As you continue in the curriculum, listen for the ways that women are treated and/or what type of work they do.

Reflection   Why might "Charlie" have made the choice he did to live as he did? What are some dangers that you have learned about from the books you have read so far about the pioneer days of early California?

The danger of bandits was very high. Because of this, stagecoach drivers were men, and dressing as a man may have helped her appear less vulnerable. Many bandits and others had guns and didn't hestitate to use them.

7.3.3   Chapters 11-12

Big Question: Are rules helpful?

1. In chapter 11, they finally reach Hangtown. As they arrive, how is it described? Where is it located? What types of trees do they notice? *It is located in the Sierras – very high up, with pine trees and icy streams.*

2. What are some of the miners' nicknames? What new names do Jack and Praiseworthy get, and why? *Some characters are Pitch-Pine Billy Pierce and Quartz Jackson. Jack gets named Jamoka Jack, as he now drinks coffee. Praiseworthy gets named Bullwhip for incident with a thief he hit uphill while on the stagecoach.*

3. What are some of the supplies they need as miners? *Miners have jackboots, colored shirts, picks and shovels, gold pans, tents, and mules.*

4. What are some methods for gold panning?
   Dry panning comes from Sonora, Mexico; dirt is scraped from a crevice, held in the air, and dropped into the other hand. The miners blow the dirt as it drops and the heavy gold remains. They also learn gold gets stuck in plant roots so they pull up plants, shake out the dirt in a pan in the stream, and the gold remains.

5. In these latest chapters, there is mention of "Miner's Law." What is a law? Look up and define it. What are some of the Miner's Laws that are mentioned? How are mining claims made? What is the consequence if Miner's Law is not followed? **Google search terms: law definition**

A law is a system of rules that are created and enforced through social or governmental institutions to regulate behavior. If you violated Miner's Law, you might be shot. Some of the Miner's Laws are:

- *As punishment for stealing, the thief's ears can be lopped off.*

- *To stake a mining claim, put 4 pegs in the ground with a can or rags on them. The claim must be worked at least 1 day a month, and defended the other 30 days.*

7.3.4   Social Status: Rich vs. Poor

Teacher's Note   This section is most relevant for grades 5-6. It lays the groundwork for later discussions in units IV and V.

Big Question: How do you know if someone is rich?

Discussion   In chapter 12, Jack realizes that Praiseworthy is attracted to his Aunt Arabella. Praiseworthy says that it would be improper for him to marry her, as he is a butler. Based on your understanding of what a butler is and who Aunt Arabella is, why would this not work?

Arabella is a wealthy landowner with servants. Praiseworthy, being a butler, is a servant. Because of these 2 facts, in those times, it would not have been proper to marry.

Rich vs. Poor Spectrum   On the rich vs. poor spectrum, how would you characterize the following characters: Jack, Pitch-Pine, and Aunt Arabella's upstairs maid?

With students, draw spectrum and fit 3 characters along it.

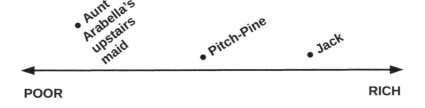

Read to Students   The idea behind this impropriety is **social status**. Social status describes the rights and privleges bestowed on people because of their economic and/or ethnic background either when they are born (ascribed), or because of their efforts (achieved).

In *Valley of the Moon*, Rosalia begins as a poor servant. As the story unfolds, the reader finds she has hidden higher social status that is only revealed when she discovers who her father is. Then she ends up significantly increasing her wealth.

In contrast, a Suisun chief would be the richest in his tribe. But he would become poorer if he went to live at a mission. He would likely lose social status if he gives up his tribal system for the Spanish system.

Written Reflection   Generally, people tend to interact with others like themselves in terms of riches and ethnicity. Think of a time when you felt uncomfortable because either people were much richer or much poorer than you. Where were you? How did you feel?

Alternative: From your experience, are there people you feel uncomfortable around? Why might you feel uncomfortable around them?

Write a paragraph in your Composition Book reflecting on either of these questions.

7.4   Week 18

7.4.1   Habitat Study: Sierra Nevadas

As Jack and Praiseworthy have ascended the mountains, they are now in a new environment, the Sierra Nevada mountain range.

Read   "Sierra Nevada Habitats" (pages 32-33) and "Effects of Glaciers" (pages 20-21) in *Audubon*.

Big Question: What causes land to change?

1. What are the names of the life zones found on mountains? *lower montane, upper montane, subalpine, and alpine zone*

2. What happens to the number of trees found as one travels up the mountain range? *As one moves from oak woodlands to the alpine zone, fewer trees are found. In the alpine zone, most plants are under 1" tall.*

3. Use Google Images to locate some photos of the Sierra Nevada habitat. Google search terms: sierra nevada california photos

4. Fill in Habitat Tracker A, table A.3 in Appendix A. Below is a key:

Habitat	Trees/Shrubs	Flowering Plants	Animals	Location (cities)
Sierra Nevada	*Giant sequoia, Sierra juniper, Jeffrey pine, Douglas fir*	*Snow plant, lupine, red heather, paintbrush*	*Bighorn sheep, hermit warblers, Douglas squirrel*	*Kirkwood, Yosemite Valley, Grant Grove*

5. Complete either the Native Habitat Home Building Project found on page 18 or fill out a Habitat Description Sheet (see table A.5). On the sheet, draw a picture of the land, a plant, and an animal and label them. Write a short paragraph about this habitat.

Sample paragraph: The Sierra Nevadas are more than 400 miles long and 40-80 miles wide. The vegetation changes dramatically with elevation. The mountain life zones are lower montane, upper montane, subalpine, and alpine. Most of the pine trees are located in the lower and upper montane zones. A visit to the alpine zone is like traveling to the tundra. Glaciers have shaped much of the Sierras. There are various forms of squirrels, which help open pinecones. Bright red snow plant can be found in the lower and upper montane zones.

7.4.2 Chapters 13-15

Big Question: How do people express who they are?

1. In Chapter 13, Jack and Praiseworthy are described as having "changed their colors to the Sierras." What does this mean? In what ways are they different from the 12-year-old boy and his butler who boarded the ship in Boston 5 months prior?

   They look like miners now and not East coasters. They wear red miner shirts, jackboots, and wide-brimmed hats. Praiseworthy has stopped shaving and he does not wear a bowler hat anymore. They live in a tent, set flea traps, and buy a squirrel gun and a mule.

2. Using answers from the previous question, reflect and fill out Jack's and Praiseworthy's Change Table (table A.19). Think about Jack's and Praiseworthy's dress, the way they speak, how they get their food, and what type of structures they live in. Below is a key.

Jack's and Praiseworthy's Change

	Before Journey (Boston)	On the Gold Fields
Praiseworthy's dress	*Wears a jacket and bowler hat*	*Red miner's shirt, wide-brimmed hat and boots*
Jack's dress	*Clothes of a wealthy East coast boy*	*Red miner's shirt, wide-brimmed hat and boots*
Home	*Large, wealthy house that had been in the family for 100 years*	*Tent*
Foods	*East coast food*	*Bear steak, coffee*
How they spend their time	*Jack was probably a student and Praiseworthy was a butler who managed servants*	*Mining, giving haricuts, shoveling coal, shooting food with their guns, pitching tent*
Other		*Learned to set flea traps*

3. When Jack goes to Cheap John's auction to buy a gun, what type of people does he see? *He sees Sonorians, Chileans, Germans, Yankees, Englishmen, and Kankas from the Sandwich Islands (Hawaii).*

4. How are the Native Americans (aka Digger Indians) choosing to spend their earnings from gold in Chapter 15? *Women buy bright calico dresses and flat woven baskets and men buy red sarapes.*

7.4.3   History: A Miner's Life Activities

Big Question: What questions do you have?

Teacher's Note   Have students choose 1-2 activities from the list below. These activities encourage student creativity in demonstrating gold rush learning thus far. With smaller writing components, the first 2 projects are simpler; the last 3 are more involved activities.

Project 1: Coming to California! Posters

East Coast steam ship operators relied on advertising posters to draw people to California. Using Google Images, explore **Google search terms: 1849 Come to California Posters**.

Discuss

1. How are the advertisers tying to "sell" people on taking the journey with them? *35- day (fast) journey; offering a quick, safe, cheap journey; superior accommodations; new ships*

2. What are the costs? *90 dollars*

3. What ports do they sail from? *New York, Boston*

Project   Have students design posters on 12x18 paper. Students should consider what unique styles of letters (fonts) they will use, and how they will encourage people to come here. Optional: www.dafont.com/ has some great decorative fonts that can be downloaded for free.

Project 2: Music

Discuss What are some words in the story used to describe gold thus far? Make a list with students. *spangles, color, gold dust, pay dirt, gold nuggets, gold fever*

Jack and Praiseworthy sing *Oh Susanna!* on the ship as they are getting close to San Francisco. Using YouTube or another online resource, listen to this song. Look at the lyrics as you listen. Lyrics can be found in Student Folder ("*Oh Susanna!* Lyrics," table A.20).

Discussion

1. From whose point of view is this song? *the miner*

2. What are some names for gold in this song? *gold dust, gold lumps, pocket full of rocks*

3. What is the general story of this miner? Where is he going? *The miner is going from Salem (Virginia) to San Francisco.*

4. What is the miner hoping for? *gold*

Project In Composition Books, students should write 2 verses of their own. To get the timing right, students can sing the verses with the tune.

Oh Susanna!
(Gold Rush Version)

I come from Salem City, with my washbowl on my knee,
I'm going to California, the gold-dust for to see.
It rained all day the day I left, the weather it was dry,
The sun so hot I froze to death – oh, brothers, don't you cry!

Chorus:
Oh, California
That's the land for me!
I'm going to San Francisco
With my washbowl on my knee.

I jumped aboard the 'Liza ship and traveled on the sea,

And every time I thought of home I wished it wasn't me!
The vessel reared like any horse, that had of oats a wealth;
I found it wouldn't throw me, so I thought I'd throw myself!

Chorus

I thought of all the pleasant times we've had together here
I thought I ort to cry a bit, but couldn't find a tear.
The pilot bread was in my mouth, the gold-dust in my eye,
And though I'm going far away, dear brothers, don't you cry!

Chorus

I soon shall be in Frisco, and there I'll look round,
And when I see the Gold lumps there I'll pick them off the ground.
I'll scrape the mountains clean, my boys.
I'll drain the rivers dry,
A pocketful of rocks bring home – so brothers, don't you cry!

Chorus

Source: Chas. F. Lummis, "Oh Susanna," in *Out West: A Magazine of the Old Pacific and the New*, Vol. XXI (July to December 1904): 271, public domain.

Project 3: Design a Miner

Discuss   From Jack's and Praiseworthy's adaptations, what have you learned about how miners live, talk, and dress? *They wear colorful shirts (sometimes checkered), jeans, hats, and boots. They create nicknames for each other.*

What items for daily living do they have with them? What tools do they use? *tents, goldpans, pick axes, guns, mules*

Project   Use Google Images to search **Google Search terms: california gold miner photos**. On a larger piece of paper (12x18), have students design their own miner, using paint, pencils, or markers. They should give their miner a creative nickname and print that name on their drawing.

Have students write 1-3 paragraphs about their imaginary miner character in Composition Books. They can consider:

1. Where their miner is from

2. How long it took to come to California, and what route their miner took

3. How successfully their miner fared

4. What is the story of how their miner got his or her nickname?

5. What techniques does their miner use in mining?

6. What mining camp does their miner live in?

Project 4: Gold! *¡Oro!*

Discuss What are some ways gold has been described in this story thus far? Make a list with students. *spangles, color, gold dust, gold nuggets, gold fever*

Activity Look on YouTube for videos of panning for gold. Go to a local stream and try it! Gold pans can be bought inexpensively online.

Written Reflection

Choice 1: Journal Article Students should write 1-2 pages in their Composition Books about their experiences gold panning. They should include the following:

1. What did they learn from watching the videos?

2. Where did they go to try?

3. How was the experience? What tecnhique did they use?

4. What did they find as they panned?

5. What would they try differently next time?

6. If a friend asked them for advice on panning, what would they tell them is the best way to do it?

Choice 2: Creative Writing   Students should imagine they are miners in 1849. Now that they have tried to pan for gold, they should create a character, and from their experience write a short story about an afternoon of gold panning. Their character can do better or worse than they did.

1. What technique did their character use?

2. What was the setting like?

3. Describe the experience panning for gold. What was the stream or soil like?

4. What will they buy with their earnings?

Project 5: Make a Mining Camp

Discussion

1. What are some mining camp names from *By the Great Horn Spoon!*? *Grizzly Flats, Chili Gulch, Hangtown, Roaring Camp*

2. Using Google, look up a few more camp names. **Google search terms: gold rush camp names**

3. Also use Google to look at photos of the camps. **Google search terms: gold rush camp photos**

4. For more camp names, look at:

http://www.malakoff.com/goldcountry/miningcampmap.gif

Project   Using recycled materials such as shoeboxes, bottled water crates, paint, and other materials, make a model of a mining camp. Think about how the miners sleep, eat, and socialize. Where would the miners hide their gold? Choose a creative name for your camp.

Writing   On an 8x5 card, write a name for camp and a short paragraph describing the camp. Affix the card to your project.

7.5 Week 19

7.5.1 Finish Miner's Life Activities

Teacher's Note Spend any time necessary to finish projects.

7.5.2 Habitat Study: Coniferous Forests

Read "Camping Out in Redwood Country," page 7 in *California Out of the Box Supplement* (*Stories from Where We Live*, page 81).

Big Question: What can we learn through field trips?

1. What types of plants and animals do they see? *They see tall redwoods, quail, chipmunks, rabbits, and abalone.*

2. How does the author describe the giant redwoods? *tall, straight, tapering, forty feet across*

3. In the last section, "Treasures of the Deep," how are the coastal trees different from the stands of redwoods they had seen at the beginning? *Due to the strong ocean wind, the pines were stunted, dwarfed, and gnarled.*

   Review Do these small, gnarled coastal trees remind you of any other twisted trees from other stories? *In* Island of the Blue Dolphins, *the island trees were small and gnarled due to the wind.*

4. Read "Coniferous Forests" (*Audubon*, pages 42-43) and "Redwood Forest" (*The California Coast* reader [*Stories from Where We Live*], page 211).

5. How many conifer species exist in California? *56*

6. Why are conifers so plentiful in California? *They have adapted to survive dry summers and fire.*

Bonus Conifers are one of the most plentiful evergreen tree varietals in the state. What areas or regions in California are conifers found in? Hint: there is a large variety of regions. Think about areas with higher elevation or copious amounts of moisture.

Redwoods are plentiful on the northwest coast; pines are common in montane areas like the Sierras; temperate rain forests are found in the extreme northwest corner of the state by the Oregon border; and Douglas firs are found above oak woodlands.

7. Use Google Images to look for pictures of the California Redwoods and Coniferous Forests. Google search terms: california redwoods coniferous tree photos

8. Fill out Habitat Tracker B (table A.4) for Coniferous Forests.

Habitat	Trees/Shrubs	Flowering Plants	Animals	Location (cities)
Coniferous Forest	*Giant Sequoia, redwoods, Jeffrey pine, Ponderosa pine*	*Ferns, club mosses, and lichens – though not true vascular plants*	*Banana slugs, California newt, northern spotted owl*	*Mendocino, Carmel, Monterey, Lake Shasta, Yosemite*

9. On your Habitat Description Sheet (table A.5), draw a picture of the land, a plant, and an animal and label them. Write a short paragraph describing the habitat. Students may opt for the Native Habitat Home Building Project described on page 18.

Sample paragraph: California features 56 species of conifers. Due to low rainfall, coastal redwood species get most of their hydration from fog as it comes in and condenses on their needles and drops moisture to the ground. The ground is surprisingly sparse, but for ferns and club mosses. Many birds, such as woodpeckers and nuthatches, bore into trees to find insects. Many other conifers, such as yellow pines, live in the lower montane regions of the Sierras.

7.5.3 Chapters 16-17

Big Question: How do we know what something is?

1. Jack and Praiseworthy follow the American River and come very close to Sutter's Mill. What happened here in 1848? *John Sutter, first mentioned in* Valley of the Moon, *hired John Marshall to build a mill. As Marshall was building the mill on the American River, he found gold.*

2. How do James Marshall and John Sutter confirm that Marshall found gold? Students will learn more about this in the next book. *They perform some rock tests. Marshall tests whether he is able to flatten gold with a rock. They also weigh gold versus silver, and run an acid test to see if the sample would corrode.*

3. Where do Jack and Praiseworthy learn the "X" is when they finally get the map from Cut-Eye Higgins? *The treasure is in the camp where they and 100 miners are – Shirt Tail Camp.*

4. In chapter 17, what do they discover as they are digging Cut-Eye Higgins grave? *gold*

5. How do Jack and Praiseworthy "stake a claim?" What does their claim look like? *They use Praiseworthy's umbrella and some sticks jack whittles. It is fifty feet wide. Praiseworthy buys a Long Tom and they run "pay dirt" through it.*

6. What does Praiseworthy leave behind when they eventually leave their claim? *Praiseworthy leaves his umbrella behind.*

Bonus/Review In Chapter 16, as Jack and Praiseworthy ride towards Sutter's Mill, they see the hillsides aglow with red and yellow. What type of habitat might they be traveling through? *chaparral or oak woodlands*

7.6 Week 20

7.6.1 Chapter 18

Big Question: Is "booklaw" an improvement? Why or why not?

1. What happens aboard their steam ship between Sacramento and San Francisco? *The boiler explodes and they are thrown into the water. So they don't sink, they drop all of their gold to the bottom of the river.*

2. What situation do they find when they get to the Long Wharf in San Francisco? What has happened with so many ships, and even the *Lady Wilma*? *They see parked ships, infested with rotting cargo, rats, and cats. Due to the lure of the gold fields, sea captians cannot find crews to operate their ships.*

3. What new scheme have they come up with to make money for their return passage to the East? What are some of the ways they have made money along the way? *They sell cats at Dr. Buckabee's auction to chase rats on ships. In this story, they have sold ties and given haircuts to make money.*

4. As they are about to book their passage back to Boston, whom do they expect to find at the wharf? How have the people from the East (Arabella) and Jack and Praiseworthy changed? How do they view their "old life" back East? What new things do they decide to do in the West? How do they plan to live?
   Jack and Praiseworthy see Aunt Arabella and Jack's sisters, Constance and Sarah. Arabella has grown tired of the old house and sold it. Praiseworthy says he has let his job as a butler go too, as he feels much more like a miner now. He asks Arabella to marry him, and she says yes. They will live in a cabin by the river.

5. What job does Praiseworthy decide he will do? Do you think his new job fits him? Why or why not? *Praiseworthy decides he will read books about law. This job does fit him, because unlike many people during that time, he can read well and is well-reasoned, as evidenced in his fight with Mountain Ox.*

6. Do you think "booklaw" was needed in California at this time? Why or why not? *Yes, booklaw was very much needed so that people would not be getting shot at or hung for stealing.*

7. Using Google, look up Marshall Gold Discovery Site (South Fork of the American River, Coloma), and add and label it on your California Map, figure B.2. **Google search terms: marshall gold discovery site map**

Reflection   If you were Jack, how would you feel about going back home after having such an adventure? What were some of your favorite parts of his journey?

Add to Timeline

- Date gold was discovered by John Marshall on the American River *January 24, 1848*

7.6.2   Land Exploration: State and National Parks

Teacher's Note   This next section provides a brief look at rich, natural places in California – state and national parks. The conclusion of this section is followed by a short consideration of naturalist John Muir. For 5th/6th grade students, you will find an optional Bonus Research Writing Project that may be used to solidify information about parks. If pressed for time, students may come back this parks section later in the curriculum.

Read to Students   Some of the great resources that California has to offer are its unique areas of wilderness. In *By the Great Horn Spoon!* you get a taste of what it was like to live in tents in the forests of the Sierras.

You have so far explored 5 habitats: coastal and island habitats, chaparral and coastal scrub, oak woodlands, sierra nevadas, and coniferous forests. Many state and national parks are nestled in these habitats.

Big Question: How do you know whether or not you like a natural area?

Overview Discussion

1. Using *Audubon*, what section and page would you turn to get information on state and national parks? *Parks and Preserves section, page 378*

   Read the Introduction to "Parks and Preserves" in *Audubon*, page 378.

2. What is the difference in designation between state and national parks? *National parks are maintained by the federal (US) government and state parks by the state of California.*

3. How many national parks are in California? *8*

4. How many national forests? *20*

5. How many state parks and beaches are in California? *200*

   Use *Audubon* (pages 378-428) as a reference for the next sections.

State Parks

1. To set the stage, use Google Images to look up **Google search terms: california state park nature photos**. What types of places do you see? *coastal areas, redwoods, poppies, rocks*

2. View this trailer for pictures of various habitats.

   California Forever Trailer
   `https://www.youtube.com/watch?v=GY72aYDNBVE`

   Notetaking Using *Audubon*, have students pick one state park that interests them. Look at photos in books or online.

   - In their Sketch Books, students should write name of state park, draw a picture of a notable feature, and note the state park habitat. Students will cover the last 3 habitats – desert, grasslands, and marshes – in the last two chapters. Find, locate, and label chosen state park on California Map (figure B.2).

National Parks

1. To get an overview, search Google search terms: california national parks nature photos. How do you describe what you see? *Examples include: large rocks of Yosemite, tall trees from Sequoia, deserts of Joshua Tree.*

2. Browse the National Park Service website for a concise list of California parks.

   ```
   https://www.nps.gov/state/ca/index.htm
   ```

3. For some of the more famous parks, visit this site:

   ```
   http://www.visitcalifornia.com/feature/9-great-national-parks
   ```

Notetaking   Which park interests you the most? In Sketch Book, title the name of the park, draw a notable feature, and note its habitat. Add and label it on California Map.

Bonus: Parks Research Writing   Pick one state or national park. Using online and/or library references, write three paragraphs about a park of student's choice. Students should cover the following details (listed in Student Folder under Parks Research, table A.21):

1. Date it became a state or national park

2. Location: what cities and freeways is it close to?

3. Activities: walking, skiing, swimming, camping, etc

4. Habitat: information about the wildlife, plants, trees

5. History: what memorable events occurred in this park?

6. Climate: rain, temperature, etc.

7. Why did you choose it? What do you like most about it?

8. Photos: include some photos of the park

7.6.3   Conservation: John Muir

Teacher's Note   A look at the state and national parks would not be complete without a brief consideration of the man known as the Father of National Parks – John Muir. He lived a significant amount of his life in California. The following videos give information about his story. Coverage of Muir is important for later discussion about water resources.

Big Question: How do you change things you don't like?

Life & Times (National Park Service Videos)

- Part 1 (10 minutes, *Biography of John Muir (part 1 of 2)*, by America Sings and produced by the National Park Service):

  https://www.youtube.com/
  watch?v=-CDzhIvugw8&feature=youtu.be

  – What are some ways he learned as a child? *He read books late at night and he walked many places.*

- Part 2 (12 minutes, Muir's later life, writing, and conservation efforts, *Biography of John Muir (2 of 2)*, by America Sings and produced by the National Park Service):

  https://www.youtube.com/watch?v=Tpgx-LkvHGE

  – What major dam project did he fight against in the last few years of his life? *He fought against the damming of Hetch Hetchy in Yosemite.*

  – What positive legacy began two years after Muir's death? *The National Park Service was created to protect natural areas such as Hetch Hetchy.*

 – Search online for recent photos of the Hetch Hetchy project. **Google search terms:** hetch hetchy dam photos

Muir's Writings

- Portrait of his writings: *Coming Home* by Michael Coleman (best for 5th/6th grade, 4 min)

  `https://vimeo.com/162323565`

Add to Timeline

- Date John Muir was born *April 21, 1838*

7.7   Week 21

7.7.1   Primary Sources: Gold Rush Stories

H R

Teacher's Note This section features 2 excerpts of stories of the California Gold Rush written by Mark Twain. The important aspect for students in hearing these stories is to listen for broad context. Twain was a vivid writer. Students may not understand all of the terms; they should listen for the "color" of the pieces themselves.

Instead of reading aloud, you may choose to listen to the noted chapters using a free audio version on Librivox by John Greenman at:

`https://librivox.org/roughing-it/`

3/4th Grade Students: Choose Excerpt 2.

1. Have students draw pictures in Sketch Books of an image they remember from the story.

2. Discuss: What do you learn about the gold rush from this story? What type of a place is California 20 years after the gold rush? *It was busy; there was gambling and lots of fights. Twenty years after the gold rush, those same towns looked like ghost towns; they were vacant.*

3. Using the IEW List of Banned Words, come up with 5 adjectives to describe the "bust" towns, and write them in Composition Book. *Bust towns: disfigured, vacant, lifeless, empty, quiet*

5/6th Grade Students: Read both excerpts. Questions are listed after the final excerpt.

Big Question: What can we learn through stories about personal experiences?

Discussion & Review Prior to Reading Selections These excerpts were written in 1870 by Mark Twain in his semi-autobiographical book, *Roughing It*. This book recounts stories from Twain's stagecoach journey from Missouri to California.

Remembering the discussion about primary and secondary sources on page 35, what can primary sources tell us that secondary (historical fiction) stories cannot? *Primary sources give the best window into how people thought during the actual time period.*

Excerpt 1: Women in the Boom

Read to Students This selection from *Roughing It* highlights the rarity of women on the gold fields.

"FETCH HER OUT."

Image source: Mark Twain, "Chapter LVII," in *Roughing It,* (Hartford, CT: American Publishing Company, 1872), accessed March 13, 2018, from www.gutenberg.org/ebooks/19033, public domain.

Chapter 57 (4:15-6:29 on Librivox)

"But they were rough in those times! They fairly reveled in gold, whisky, fights, and fandangoes, and were unspeakably happy. The honest miner raked from a hundred to a thousand dollars out of his claim a day, and what with the gambling dens and the other entertainments, he hadn't a cent the next morning, if he had any sort of luck. They cooked their own bacon and beans, sewed on their own buttons, washed their own shirts–blue woollen ones; and if a man wanted a fight on his hands without any annoying delay, all he had to do was to appear in public in a white shirt or a stove-pipe hat, and he would be accommodated. For those people hated aristocrats. They had a particular and malignant animosity toward what they called a "biled shirt."

It was a wild, free, disorderly, grotesque society! Men–only swarming hosts of stalwart men–nothing juvenile, nothing feminine, visible anywhere!

In those days miners would flock in crowds to catch a glimpse of that rare and blessed spectacle, a woman! Old inhabitants tell how, in a certain camp, the news went abroad early in the morning that a woman was come! They had seen a calico dress hanging out of a wagon down at the camping-ground–sign of emigrants from over the great plains. Everybody went down there, and a shout went up when an actual, bona fide dress was discovered fluttering in the wind! The male emigrant was visible. The miners said:

"Fetch her out!"

He said: "It is my wife, gentlemen–she is sick–we have been robbed of money, provisions, everything, by the Indians–we want to rest."

"Fetch her out! We've got to see her!"

"But, gentlemen, the poor thing, she–"

"FETCH HER OUT!"

He "fetched her out," and they swung their hats and sent up three rousing cheers and a tiger; and they crowded around and gazed at her, and touched her dress, and listened to her voice with the look of men who listened to a memory rather than a present reality–and then they collected twenty-five hundred dollars in gold and gave it to the man, and swung their hats again and gave three more cheers, and went home satisfied."

Source: Mark Twain, "Chapter LVII," in *Roughing It,* (Hartford, CT: American Publishing Company, 1872), accessed March 13, 2018, from www.gutenberg.org/ebooks/19033, public domain.

Excerpt 2: And Bust!

Chapter 57 (0-4:15 on Librivox)

Read to Students   How does California look 20 years after the gold rush? Find out in this final excerpt from *Roughing It.*

"It was in this Sacramento Valley, just referred to, that a deal of the most lucrative of the early gold mining was done, and you may still see, in places, its grassy slopes and levels torn and guttered and disfigured by the avaricious spoilers of fifteen and twenty years ago. You may see such disfigurements far and wide over California–and in some such places, where only meadows and forests are visible–not a living creature, not a house, no stick or stone or remnant of a ruin, and not a sound, not even a whisper to disturb the Sabbath stillness–you will find it hard to believe that there stood at one time a fiercely-flourishing little city, of two thousand or three thousand souls, with its newspaper, fire company, brass band, volunteer militia, bank, hotels, noisy Fourth of July processions and speeches, gambling hells crammed with tobacco smoke, profanity, and rough-bearded men of all nations

and colors, with tables heaped with gold dust sufficient for the
revenues of a German principality–streets crowded and rife with
business–town lots worth four hundred dollars a front foot–labor,
laughter, music, dancing, swearing, fighting, shooting, stabbing–a
bloody inquest and a man for breakfast every morning–everything
that delights and adorns existence–all the appointments and ap-
purtenances of a thriving and prosperous and promising young
city,–and now nothing is left of it all but a lifeless, homeless solitude. The men are gone, the houses have vanished, even the name
of the place is forgotten. In no other land, in modern times, have
towns so absolutely died and disappeared, as in the old mining
regions of California.

It was a driving, vigorous, restless population in those days. It
was a curious population. It was the only population of the kind
that the world has ever seen gathered together, and it is not likely
that the world will ever see its like again. For observe, it was an
assemblage of two hundred thousand young men–not simpering,
dainty, kid-gloved weaklings, but stalwart, muscular, dauntless
young braves, brimful of push and energy, and royally endowed
with every attribute that goes to make up a peerless and magnificent manhood–the very pick and choice of the world's glorious
ones. No women, no children, no gray and stooping veterans,–
none but erect, bright-eyed, quick-moving, strong-handed young
giants–the strangest population, the finest population, the most
gallant host that ever trooped down the startled solitudes of an
unpeopled land. And where are they now? Scattered to the
ends of the earth–or prematurely aged and decrepit–or shot or
stabbed in street affrays–or dead of disappointed hopes and broken hearts–all gone, or nearly all–victims devoted upon the altar
of the golden calf–the noblest holocaust that ever wafted its sac-
rificial incense heavenward. It is pitiful to think upon.

It was a splendid population–for all the slow, sleepy, sluggish-
brained sloths staid at home–you never find that sort of people
among pioneers–you cannot build pioneers out of that sort of material. It was that population that gave to California a name for

getting up astounding enterprises and rushing them through with a magnificent dash and daring and a recklessness of cost or consequences, which she bears unto this day–and when she projects a new surprise, the grave world smiles as usual, and says "Well, that is California all over."

Source: Mark Twain, "Chapter LVII," in *Roughing It,* (Hartford, CT: American Publishing Company, 1872), accessed March 13, 2018, from www.gutenberg.org/ebooks/19033, public domain.

5th/6th Grade Discussion

1. From this final passage, what type of a place was California 20 years after 1849? *California was like a ghost town, people and houses were gone, and even the place names had disappeared.*

2. What adjectives does Twain use to describe people living on the gold fields? What type of people were they? *They were strong, curious, vigorous, restless, stalwart, muscular, driving, dauntless, and brave. He describes them as strong young men – no women, children, or older men.*

3. What are some qualities of this "pioneer spirit?" *determined, energetic, brave*

4. Remembering back to the discussion of primary and secondary sources, what type of a source are the excerpts from *Roughing It*? Why? Roughing It *is a primary source because Twain wrote this during his own time period using the experience of his own journeys.*

5. What do you learn from this source about California that you would not from other types of sources? *In this source, he gives a vivid, rich picture of the miners. One can just imagine being there with the miners!*

7.7.2   Social Science: Population after the Gold Rush

Teacher's Note   In this section, using an open source, free, online encyclopedia – Wikipedia – students will explore the population growth post-gold rush.

Big Question: What could someone hear that might motivate them to move?

Read to Students   In *By the Great Horn Spoon!* and *Roughing It*, you see various mentions of many new people coming to strike it rich. You will use Wikipedia to trace how the California population grows after the gold rush.

1. Enter Google search terms: wikipedia california population chart

2. Enter total population numbers in California Population Growth (1850-1900) Chart, table A.22 in Appendix A. Also, enter the corresponding growth rates for those years.

Answer key:

California Population Growth (1850-1900)

Year	Population	Growth Rate
1850	*92,597*	–
1860	*379,994*	*310.4%*
1870	*560,247*	*47.4%*
1880	*864,694*	*54.3%*
1890	*1,213,398*	*40.3%*
1900	*1,485,053*	*22.4%*

1. Looking at your completed chart, what do you think a growth rate means? *The growth rate is the rate of change in a value over a period of time. In this case, it is the increase or decrease in the population size.*

2. What 10-year period had the highest growth rate? What decade (or 10-year period) had the lowest growth rate? *The highest growth rate is from 1850-1860, at 310%. The lowest growth rate occurs from 1890 to 1900, at 22%.*

3. What do you think might explain the highest growth decade in the population? *From 1850 to 1860, many were coming to look for gold.*

7.8 Week 22

7.8.1 Technology: Speedy Delivery of News and People

Pony Express – Got to get the mail through!

Big Question: How has communication changed over time? (Murdoch, 2015)

Discuss What ways have you learned about how news and information traveled in California's early years? *Pigeon Express, telegraph*

Read to Students In 1860, a new method of delivering mail was devised – the Pony Express! Young hardy riders carried mail on horseback from St. Joseph, Missouri to Sacramento. The journey took 10 days. The service continued for eighteen months. The Pony Express operators pressed to get a government contract for their work, but the answer came too late. And, as you will shortly see, other methods of viable, fast travel were in the exploratory stages.

Here is Mark Twain's account of seeing a Pony Express rider while on a stagecoach journey. While reading selection, you may look at the map of the Pony Express (figures B.11, B.12, and B.13).

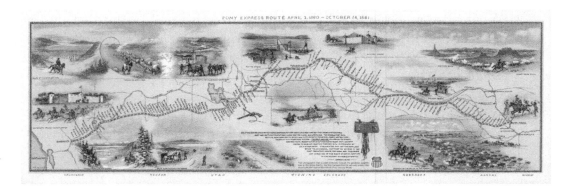

Source: William Henry Jackson, "Pony Express Map William Henry Jackson.jpg," *Wikimedia Commons*, accessed June 23, 2018, https://commons.wikimedia.org/w/index.php?curid=10111804, public domain.

Chapter 8   (0-4:44 on Librivox)

In a little while all interest was taken up in stretching our necks and watching for the "pony-rider"–the fleet messenger who sped across the continent from St. Joe to Sacramento, carrying letters nineteen hundred miles in eight days! Think of that for perishable horse and human flesh and blood to do! The pony-rider was usually a little bit of a man, brimful of spirit and endurance. No matter what time of the day or night his watch came on, and no matter whether it was winter or summer, raining, snowing, hailing, or sleeting, or whether his "beat" was a level straight road or a crazy trail over mountain crags and precipices, or whether it led through peaceful regions or regions that swarmed with hostile Indians, he must be always ready to leap into the saddle and be off like the wind! There was no idling-time for a pony-rider on duty. He rode fifty miles without stopping, by daylight, moonlight, starlight, or through the blackness of darkness–just as it happened. He rode a splendid horse that was born for a racer and fed and lodged like a gentleman; kept him at his utmost speed for ten miles, and then, as he came crashing up to the station where stood two men holding fast a fresh, impatient steed, the transfer of rider and mail-bag was made in the twinkling of an eye, and away flew the eager pair and were out of sight before the spectator could get hardly the ghost of a look. Both rider and horse went "flying light." The rider's dress was thin, and fitted close; he wore a "round-about," and a skull-cap, and tucked his pantaloons into his boot-tops like a race-rider. He carried no arms–he carried nothing that was not absolutely necessary, for even the postage on his literary freight was worth five dollars a letter.

f a racing-sad-
blanket. He
r none at all.
-pockets strap-

"HERE HE COMES."

Image source: Mark Twain, "Chapter VIII," in *Roughing It*, (Hartford, CT: American Publishing Company, 1872), accessed June 21, 2018, from www.gutenberg.org/ebooks/19033, public domain.

He got but little frivolous correspondence to carry–his bag had business letters in it, mostly. His horse was stripped of all unnecessary weight, too. He wore a little wafer of a racing-saddle, and no visible blanket. He wore light shoes, or none at all. The little flat mail-pockets strapped under the rider's thighs would each hold about the bulk of a child's primer. They held many and many an important business chapter and newspaper letter, but these were written on paper as airy and thin as gold-leaf, nearly, and thus bulk and weight were economized. The stage-coach traveled about a hundred to a hundred and twenty-five miles a day (twenty-four hours), the pony-rider about two hundred and fifty. There were about eighty pony-riders in the saddle all the time, night and day, stretching in a long, scattering procession from

Missouri to California, forty flying eastward, and forty toward the west, and among them making four hundred gallant horses earn a stirring livelihood and see a deal of scenery every single day in the year.

We had had a consuming desire, from the beginning, to see a pony-rider, but somehow or other all that passed us and all that met us managed to streak by in the night, and so we heard only a whiz and a hail, and the swift phantom of the desert was gone before we could get our heads out of the windows. But now we were expecting one along every moment, and would see him in broad daylight. Presently the driver exclaims:

"HERE HE COMES!"

Every neck is stretched further, and every eye strained wider. Away across the endless dead level of the prairie a black speck appears against the sky, and it is plain that it moves. Well, I should think so!

In a second or two it becomes a horse and rider, rising and falling, rising and falling–sweeping toward us nearer and nearer–growing more and more distinct, more and more sharply defined–nearer and still nearer, and the flutter of the hoofs comes faintly to the ear–another instant a whoop and a hurrah from our upper deck, a wave of the rider's hand, but no reply, and man and horse burst past our excited faces, and go winging away like a belated fragment of a storm!

CHANGING HORSES.

Image source: Mark Twain, "Chapter VIII," in *Roughing It,* (Hartford, CT: American Publishing Company, 1872), accessed June 21, 2018, from www.gutenberg.org/ebooks/19033, public domain.

So sudden is it all, and so like a flash of unreal fancy, that but for the flake of white foam left quivering and perishing on a mail-sack after the vision had flashed by and disappeared, we might have doubted whether we had seen any actual horse and man at all, maybe.

Source: Mark Twain, "Chapter VIII," in *Roughing It,* (Hartford, CT: American Publishing Company, 1872), accessed June 21, 2018, from www.gutenberg.org/ebooks/19033, public domain.

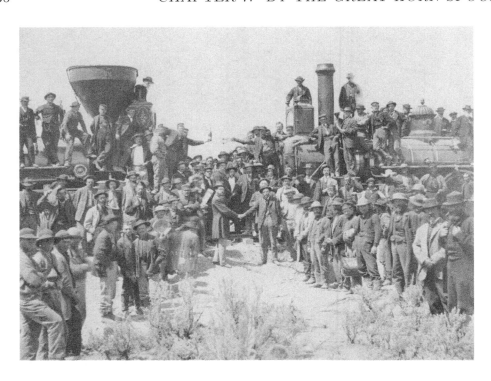

Source: Andrew J. Russell, "East and West Shaking Hands at the Laying of the Last Rail of the Union Pacific Railroad.jpg," *Wikimedia Commons*, accessed June 20, 2018, https://commons.wikimedia.org/wiki/File:East_and_West_Shaking_hands_at_the_laying_of_last_rail_Union_Pacific_Railroad_-_Restoration.jpg, public domain.

Transcontinental Railroad - Done!

Big Question: What makes a trip a good trip?

Discuss Looking at table A.22, after 1850, how do you imagine people came to California?

How had people come previously to California? *They came by boat, overland in covered wagons through the Sierras, or on foot from Mexico.*

Reader's Theater: Visit the National Park Service Website link below. Teacher and students will read together, "The Last Spike is Driven" (a Reenactment Script for the Golden Spike Ceremony). Divide up the roles and read dialogue about the Golden Spike ceremony.

```
https://www.nps.gov/gosp/learn/
kidsyouth/re-enactment-script-grades-4-6.htm
```

Another good site containing the dialogue from the Golden Spike ceremony is the Central Pacific Railroad Photographic History Museum.

```
http://cprr.org/Museum/Done!.html
```

Read and Discuss   These were the words that came across the telegraph on May 10, 1869 from Promontory Summit, Utah.

The Central Pacific (from Sacramento, California) and Union Pacific (from Omaha, Nebraska/Council Bluffs, Iowa) nailed in the last spike – the Golden Spike. The east and west coasts were now linked by way of rail. Other established lines would take passengers from Omaha, Nebraska to the East Coast. Now, in 8-10 days time, a person could travel from New York to Sacramento in coach class comfort.

Compared to other forms of transportation, what were some dangers they could avoid by taking the train? *bandits and many days spent in a hot, dusty stagecoach*

In *Roughing It*, Mark Twain recounts a sketch from the *New York Times* of a ride on the new railway.

Chapter 4   (16:38-19:52 on Librivox)

> Now that was stage-coaching on the great overland, ten or twelve years ago, when perhaps not more than ten men in America, all told, expected to live to see a railroad follow that route to the Pacific. But the railroad is there, now, and it pictures a thousand odd comparisons and contrasts in my mind to read the following sketch, in the *New York Times*, of a recent trip over almost the very ground I have been describing. I can scarcely comprehend

the new state of things:

"ACROSS THE CONTINENT.

"At 4.20 P.M., Sunday, we rolled out of the station at Omaha, and started westward on our long jaunt. A couple of hours out, dinner was announced–an "event" to those of us who had yet to experience what it is to eat in one of Pullman's hotels on wheels; so, stepping into the car next forward of our sleeping palace, we found ourselves in the dining-car. It was a revelation to us, that first dinner on Sunday. And though we continued to dine for four days, and had as many breakfasts and suppers, our whole party never ceased to admire the perfection of the arrangements, and the marvelous results achieved. Upon tables covered with snowy linen, and garnished with services of solid silver, Ethiop waiters, flitting about in spotless white, placed as by magic a repast at which Delmonico himself could have had no occasion to blush; and, indeed, in some respects it would be hard for that distinguished chef to match our menu; for, in addition to all that ordinarily makes up a first-chop dinner, had we not our antelope steak (the gormand who has not experienced this–bah! what does he know of the feast of fat things?) our delicious mountain-brook trout, and choice fruits and berries, and (sauce piquant and un-purchasable!) our sweet-scented, appetite-compelling air of the prairies?

"You may depend upon it, we all did justice to the good things, and as we washed them down with bumpers of sparkling Krug, whilst we sped along at the rate of thirty miles an hour, agreed it was the fastest living we had ever experienced. (We beat that, however, two days afterward when we made twenty-seven miles in twenty-seven minutes, while our Champagne glasses filled to the brim spilled not a drop!) After dinner we repaired to our drawing-room car, and, as it was Sabbath eve, intoned some of the grand old hymns— "Praise God from whom," etc.; "Shining Shore," "Coronation," etc. – the voices of the men singers and of the women singers blending sweetly in the evening air, while our train, with its great, glaring Polyphemus eye, lighting up long vistas of prairie, rushed into the night and the Wild. Then to bed in luxurious couches, where we slept the sleep of the just and only awoke the next morning (Monday) at eight o'clock, to find ourselves at the crossing of the North Platte, three hundred miles from Omaha–fifteen hours and forty minutes out."

Source: Mark Twain, "Chapter IV," in *Roughing It,* (Hartford, CT: American Publishing Company, 1872), accessed June 21, 2018, from www.gutenberg.org/ebooks/19033, public domain.

Video The following, *America: The Story of Us*, is a brief 3:30 movie about the building of the transcontinental railroad found on the History Channel site. Note: Teacher should preview video first as it shows the dangers the Chinese faced in building the railroad.

```
https://www.history.com/shows/america-the-story-of-us/videos/
transcontinental-railroad
```

Discuss

- What ethnicity encompassed two-thirds of the workforce? *Chinese*

- What motivated many Americans to travel out west? *land grants*

- Using the Transcontinental Railroad Map (figure B.14 in Appendix B), label Promontory Summit (Utah), Sacramento (California), and Omaha (Nebraska)/Council Bluffs, (Iowa). Label the states the railroad passes through.

- Also, color and label the Central Pacific line (from #1-2) one color. Color and label the Unionl Pacific Railroad (#2-3) in another color.

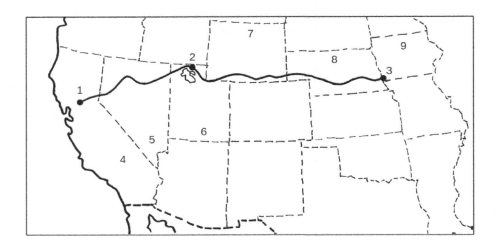

Answer key:

1. Sacramento, CA

2. Promontory Summit, Utah

3. Omaha, Nebraska/Council Bluffs, Iowa

4. California

5. Nevada

6. Utah

7. Wyoming

8. Nebraska

9. Iowa

- If you had the choice of covered wagon, stagecoach, Pony Express, train, or boat – which way would you choose to travel to California?

Add to Timeline

- Years of the Pony Express *1860-61*

- Date Transcontinental Railroad completed *May 10, 1869*

7.8.2   End of Unit III Questions

Questions for further consideration:

1. What questions do you have?

2. What types of mining have you learned about thus far? What are some challenges to each of the methods? Which takes the longest?

   Methods include: gold panning (swirling dirt in pan), dry panning from Sonora (holding dry dirt up and blowing dirt away so gold remains), and mining in a Long Tom (putting dirt in box with running water and the gold gets stuck). Sonoran minning takes the longest.

   Look at this site for more techniques:

   `https://www.sierracollege.edu/`
   `ejournals/jsnhb/v2n1/miningtechniques.html`

   Choose 1 new technique and write either instructions or a paragraph about how a miner would look for gold using this technique. Draw a picture to illustrate method in Sketch Book.

   Sample paragraph:
   Dredging: using boats to send buckets down as much as 100 feet under the level of surface water, material is gathered to be processed. The gravel is screened out and washed to separate gold from gravel. The heavy material is put into barrels where copper plates trap the gold. Gravel waste is dumped to form tailings. This method was most popular at the turn of the 20th century.

3. **Part 1:** The character of María Rosalia lived during the same time period as *By The Great Horn Spoon!* How might she feel living at one of the mining camps, and not on the Medina rancho? What was it like to be a woman/girl in these times? How were women treated in *Roughing It* and "The Secret of CD Parkhurst"?

It would be difficult for Rosalia to live at a mining camp, as there were no women or children there. Even though life was harder as a servant girl, she would probably be more comfortable on the rancho, as food and housing were better. In "CD Parkhurst," Charlie had to dress up as a man to safely drive a stagecoach. In Roughing It, *a woman was such a novelty on the gold fields, a woman could almost be paid for showing her face.*

Part 2: How could María Rosalia make it as a "49er"? Write a story about how she does it! How does she come to the fields, get around, mine for gold, and defend herself? What businesses could she be involved with and who might be her friends? What skills might she bring to her work? (Hint: students may need to review charts such as tables A.15 and B.9, as well as any other selections in Student Folder).

Encourage students to consider a "CD Parkhurst" approach, where their female character goes incognito. Imagine the character comes up with a miner's nickname and lives in one of the mining camps. Imagine she brings her knowledge of farming and reading and, like Praiseworthy, gets ahead and finds opportunity.

4. **Part 1:** How might the character of Karana do on the gold fields? Think about how Native Americans were viewed by the miners in *By The Great Horn Spoon!* According to the miners, what did the "Digger Indians" do with their mining earnings? How might the Native American way of life change with all the new ethnicities that came to California?

Karana would probably be wowed by the technology of the riverboat and stagecoaches. She might try her hand at gold and maybe buy western clothing with her earnings. She might still live with her tribe, if she found any remnants of her tribe alive. She would probably not mix with the other cultures.

Part 2: Instead of being taken to the Santa Barbara Mission after 18 years alone on San Nicolas Island, imagine she goes to the gold fields. What new technology does she see? What is she amazed by and scared of? Imagine you are writing from her perspective, and write 2-3 aspects of life on the gold fields that she either likes or does not like.

She would be scared of all of the guns and theft. She might meet other Native Americans, live with them, and try gold panning as they do, though she could not speak with them. She would not go out alone, as it was not safe for women.

5. Imagine you lived in the 1800s in California. If you lived during the times of these 3 characters we have explored – Karana, María Rosalia, and Jack, which of these three would you want to live like? What part of California would you live in? What type of housing would you build? What type of foods would you eat, and how would you make and obtain your food? What would you do each day? What is your habitat like – plants, trees, rocks, and animals?

Pick a character name that suits you. Write about your life from the perspective of this person.

Characters & Habitats Key:

- *María Rosalia: rancho in oak woodlands/chaparral/marsh habitat*
- *Karana: lived on Channel Island in islands habitat*
- *Jack: journeyed from Boston to California to Sierra Nevada habitat*

6. Like Jack Flagg, you are bound for San Francisco from Boston by ship. Create a slideshow presentation of pictures of the journey. Do you go through the Cape, the straits, or the Panama Canal? Use your Map of the Americas (figure B.10) to remember the places you have gone. Come up with a script telling your viewers where you went, what you saw, and what the weather was like.

See Map of the Americas Key, in Appendix C for possible locations.

7. What modes of transportation have you read about? *boats, pony express, stagecoach, train*

   Look into the mode that's your favorite, and find five facts to report.

Unit IV

¡Terremoto!

(Earthquake)

California Jolted:
The San Francisco Earthquake

Chapter 8

Unit Introduction

8.1 Supplies for This Unit

1. Resources used throughout

   - See list on page 2

2. Chapter 9: *The Earth Dragon Awakes*

   - *The Earth Dragon Awakes* (Laurence Yep, ISBN 978-0-06-000846-8)

   - Library reference book on the Earth from the children's section, such as *Earth* by Susanna Van Rose (DK Eyewitness Books) or *Super Earth Encyclopedia* by John Woodward (Smithsonian)

   - Drawing chalk and pencil

   - Crayons or colored pencils

   - Various materials depending on project for "A Closer Look: Using Figurative Language," page 164

   - Gardening gloves

   - Sharpie marker

   - Masking tape

   - Steel file or quartz rock

   - 10-16 rocks

- Safety goggles
- Old towel
- Hammer
- Two handtowels
- Optional: materials for Native Habitat Home Design in "Habitat Study: Coast and Islands," page 18

8.2 Week 23

8.2.1 Weather: San Francisco & Beyond

Read to Students In this next section, you will come back to a place you have been once before – where you left Jack and Praiseworthy – in the city of San Francisco.

Read "Fog – San Francisco," on page 80 in *The California Coast* reader (*Stories from Where We Live*), and "The Real Work," link in *California Out of the Box Supplement* (*Stories from Where We Live*, page 10).

Big Question: In a natural area, why is the amount of rain or moisture important?

1. What types of weather are mentioned? What different animals appear in these poems? *Weather includes: fog, haze, sun. Animals include: sea lions, birds, seagulls, mountain lion (paws), snake (tail).*

2. Use Google Images to look for some pictures of San Francisco. What landmarks do you observe? What style of buildings do you see? **Google search terms: san francisco photos**
   There are lots of photos of the red Golden Gate Bridge and Victorian style homes. There is also a modern downtown.

3. Also, look for some Google Images of San Francisco fog. In your Sketch Book, using either pencil or drawing chalk, sketch one of your favorite pictures of the fog. **Google search terms: san francisco fog photos**

   Read "Typical Clouds" in *Audubon*, pages 64 and 65.

4. From your reading, what type of clouds are fog? How are clouds formed? Which type of clouds are your favorite? *Fog is merely clouds formed at ground level. Clouds are formed when moist air is cooled, causing water molecules to condense into water droplets or ice crystals.*

Rainfall and Population Patterns

Teacher's Note   This next section is appropriate for advanced 4th and 5th-6th grades. The most difficult aspect will be finding the sources of data. If ranking the population and precipitation proves too difficult, have students discuss information.

Read to Students   Now you will spend some time exploring rain or precipitation levels. Find your California Map (figure B.2) or refer to your Mapmaker map of California. Using Google Images, find a map that shows average annual precipitation levels for California. **Google search terms: california average precipitation map**

The following link features a helpful map. Print it out and have students keep it in Student Folder. (It will be used later in "Natural Resource: Water," beginning on page 183.)

```
http://www.eldoradocountyweather.com/
californiaannualprecip.html
```

Average Annual Precipitation & Population

Note: Answers will vary somewhat depending on weather and population charts used.

City	Precipitation	Rank	Population	Rank
	Year: *1900-1960*		Year: *1960*	
Sacramento	*17"*	2	*191,667*	4
San Francisco	*17"*	2	*740,316*	2
Santa Barbara	*14-15"*	3	*58,768*	6
Monterey	*17"*	2	*22,618*	9
Los Angeles	*14-15"*	3	*2,479,015*	1
San Diego	*9-11"*	4	*573,224*	3
#1: Eureka	*37.5"*	1	*28,137*	8
#2: Bakersfield	*4-6.5"*	6	*56,848*	7
#3: Fresno	*9"*	5	*133,929*	5

1. Fill in the Average Annual Precipitation & Population Chart, table A.23 in Appendix A, and note the annual average precipitation for each of these cities from your map. Make a note of the year of your data in the year box.

2. Choose 3 other cities that are located in areas of *significantly* lower or higher rainfall than these cities and add these cities, and precipitation levels to your chart in boxes #1-3.

3. Rank the cities' precipitation, with 1 as the highest, and 9 as the lowest. If cities have the same rainfall, give them all the same ranking number.

4. What areas get the most precipitation? How many inches do they get? What areas get the least, and how many inches of rain do they receive? Color the highest rainfall box green, and the lowest rainfall box red. *Eureka, Sacramento, SF, and Monterey all get more rain. They get 37.5-17" of rain. Bakersfield and Fresno get the lowest amount of rain, at 4-9."*

5. Now, using the California Department of Finance data:

   ```
   www.dof.ca.gov/Reports/Demographic.../
   2010-1850_STCO_IncCities-FINAL.xls
   ```

   Look up the population during the **corresponding time period** for the cities on the chart, and add those population numbers. If your chosen cities are very small cities, you may need to look up the population number directly in Wikipedia for that year. Take care that the population numbers all come from the same year. **Google search terms: california historical population patterns**

6. Rank the cities in terms of population size, with the largest city being 1, and the smallest city 9.

7. What city in your chart has the largest population? Lowest? Color the largest population box green, and the smallest box red. *In this chart, Los Angeles has the highest population and Monterey has the lowest population.*

8. In the city with the highest population, what is the rainfall level? *Los Angeles has highest population, but rainfall in the middle range.*

9. In the city with the greatest amount of rainfall, what is the population? *Eureka has the highest rainfall, but the second smallest population.*

10. What about the city with the lowest rainfall? What is the population? *In Bakersfield, which has the lowest rainfall, the population is the third smallest.*

11. What level of rain do you prefer, and why? *Answers will vary.*

Bonus   What population pattern do you notice about areas with little rainfall? Do these areas have a large or small population? How about the population size for areas with higher rainfall? And population size for rainfall in the middle? *Cities with the highest and lowest rainfall have smaller populations. Cities that have rainfall levels in the middle have the largest populations.*

Bonus   Why might people choose not to settle in cities with lower rainfall levels? And why might population be lower in cities with the most rainfall? *It may be harder to establish cities in areas with less rain; water might be more expensive in desert areas. More people want to live where their is enough water, but not too much. Also, if the rainfall levels are high, the area might be more remote, and it would be hard to start a huge city in that location.*

8.2.2   Mark Twain and the "Great" Earthquake in San Francisco

---

Teacher's Note   Encourage students to listen to this section for literary color and flavor. You may choose to listen to this excerpt on Librivox.

```
https://librivox.org/roughing-it/
```

Read to Students   In Mark Twain's *Roughing It*, during his time in San Francisco, he recounts an earthquake experience on October 8, 1865.

Chapter 58   (4:26-11:45 on Librivox)

A month afterward I enjoyed my first earthquake. It was one which was long called the "great" earthquake, and is doubtless so distinguished till this day. It was just after noon, on a bright October day. I was coming down Third street. The only objects in motion anywhere in sight in that thickly built and populous quarter, were a man in a buggy behind me, and a street car wending slowly up the cross street. Otherwise, all was solitude and a Sabbath stillness. As I turned the corner, around a frame house, there was a great rattle and jar, and it occurred to me that here was an item! —no doubt a fight in that house. Before I could turn and seek the door, there came a really terrific shock; the ground seemed to roll under me in waves, interrupted by a violent joggling up and down, and there was a heavy grinding noise as of brick houses rubbing together. I fell up against the frame house and hurt my elbow. I knew what it was, now, and from mere reportorial instinct, nothing else, took out my watch and noted the time of day; at that moment a third and still severer shock came, and as I reeled about on the pavement trying to keep my footing, I saw a sight! The entire front of a tall four-story brick building in Third street sprung outward like a door and fell sprawling across the street, raising a dust like a great volume of smoke! And here came the buggy—overboard went the man, and in less time than I can tell it the vehicle was distributed in small fragments along three hundred yards of street.

Image source: Mark Twain, "Chapter LVIII," in *Roughing It* (Hartford, CT: American Publishing Company, 1872), accessed March 13, 2018, from www.gutenberg.org/ebooks/19033, public domain.

One could have fancied that somebody had fired a charge of chair-rounds and rags down the thoroughfare. The street car had stopped, the horses were rearing and plunging, the passengers were pouring out at both ends, and one fat man had crashed half way through a glass window on one side of the car, got wedged fast and was squirming and screaming like an impaled madman. Every door, of every house, as far as the eye could reach, was vomiting a stream of human beings; and almost before one could execute a wink and begin another, there was a massed multitude of people stretching in endless procession down every street my position commanded. Never was solemn solitude turned into teeming life quicker.

Of the wonders wrought by "the great earthquake," these were all that came under my eye; but the tricks it did, elsewhere, and far and wide over the town, made toothsome gossip for nine days.

The destruction of property was trifling–the injury to it was widespread and somewhat serious.

The "curiosities" of the earthquake were simply endless. Gentlemen and ladies who were sick, or were taking a siesta, or had dissipated till a late hour and were making up lost sleep, thronged into the public streets in all sorts of queer apparel, and some without any at all. One woman who had been washing a naked child, ran down the street holding it by the ankles as if it were a dressed turkey. Prominent citizens who were supposed to keep the Sabbath strictly, rushed out of saloons in their shirt-sleeves, with billiard cues in their hands. Dozens of men with necks swathed in napkins, rushed from barber-shops, lathered to the eyes or with one cheek clean shaved and the other still bearing a hairy stubble. Horses broke from stables, and a frightened dog rushed up a short attic ladder and out on to a roof, and when his scare was over had not the nerve to go down again the same way he had gone up.

A prominent editor flew down stairs, in the principal hotel, with nothing on but one brief undergarment-met a chambermaid, and exclaimed:

"Oh, what shall I do! Where shall I go!" She responded with naive serenity:

"If you have no choice, you might try a clothing-store!"

A certain foreign consul's lady was the acknowledged leader of fashion, and every time she appeared in anything new or extraordinary, the ladies in the vicinity made a raid on their husbands' purses and arrayed themselves similarly. One man who had suffered considerably and growled accordingly, was standing at the window when the shocks came, and the next instant the consul's wife, just out of the bath, fled by with no other apology for clothing than-a bath-towel! The sufferer rose superior to the terrors of the earthquake, and said to his wife:

"Now that is something like! Get out your towel my dear!"

The plastering that fell from ceilings in San Francisco that day, would have covered several acres of ground. For some days afterward, groups of eyeing and pointing men stood about many a building, looking at long zig-zag cracks that extended from the eaves to the ground. Four feet of the tops of three chimneys on one house were broken square off and turned around in such a way as to completely stop the draft.

A crack a hundred feet long gaped open six inches wide in the middle of one street and then shut together again with such force, as to ridge up the meeting earth like a slender grave. A lady sitting in her rocking and quaking parlor, saw the wall part at the ceiling, open and shut twice, like a mouth, and then drop the end of a brick on the floor like a tooth. She was a woman easily disgusted with foolishness, and she arose and went out of there. One lady who was coming down stairs was astonished to see a bronze Hercules lean forward on its pedestal as if to strike her with its club. They both reached the bottom of the flight at the same time,–the woman insensible from the fright. Her child, born some little time afterward, was club-footed. However-on second thought,–if the reader sees any coincidence in this, he must do it at his own risk.

The first shock brought down two or three huge organ-pipes in one of the churches. The minister, with uplifted hands, was just closing the services. He glanced up, hesitated, and said:

"However, we will omit the benediction!"–and the next instant there was a vacancy in the atmosphere where he had stood.

After the first shock, an Oakland minister said:

"Keep your seats! There is no better place to die than this"--

And added, after the third:

"But outside is good enough!" He then skipped out at the back door.

Such another destruction of mantel ornaments and toilet bottles as the earthquake created, San Francisco never saw before. There was hardly a girl or a matron in the city but suffered losses of this kind. Suspended pictures were thrown down, but oftener still, by a curious freak of the earthquake's humor, they were whirled completely around with their faces to the wall! There was great difference of opinion, at first, as to the course or direction the earthquake traveled, but water that splashed out of various tanks and buckets settled that. Thousands of people were made so sea-sick by the rolling and pitching of floors and streets that they were weak and bed-ridden for hours, and some few for even days afterward.--Hardly an individual escaped nausea entirely.

The queer earthquake--episodes that formed the staple of San Francisco gossip for the next week would fill a much larger book than this, and so I will diverge from the subject.

Source: Mark Twain, "Chapter LVIII," in *Roughing It* (Hartford, CT: American Publishing Company, 1872), accessed March 13, 2018, from www.gutenberg.org/ebooks/19033, public domain.

Bonus/Review The city of San Francisco is mentioned in *Valley of the Moon* as well, except it had another name at that point in history. What was the initial name? Do some brief research on when the name changed.

Google search terms: san francisco name history

Its initial name was Yerba Buena, which is the name of a trailing evergreen herb with small white flowers; the city got the name San Francisco in 1847 because of the Mission San Francisco de Asís. Today Yerba Buena is a neighborhood in San Francisco.

8.2.3   An Even Greater Earthquake, San Francisco, 1906

> **Teacher's Note**   Normally, in this curriculum, students read each chapter book and incorporate science as they read each story. This unit follows a different pattern as students will read and finish the book first, and then look at the science behind earthquakes.

Read to Students   The next book you will read, also about San Francisco, follows an Anglo (white) family and a Chinese immigrant family at the time of the Great Earthquake of 1906. At this time, San Francisco had the largest population of any California city.

As you read, listen for two things:

1. What is going on below the Earth's surface?

2. How is the situation different for the Chinese family versus the white family?

Chapter 9

The Earth Dragon Awakes

9.1 Week 24

9.1.1 Pages 1-18

Big Question: What's beneath our feet and why does it matter? (Murdoch, 2015)

1. What year does this story start in? *1906*

2. How long has it been since the last earthquake? *38 years*

3. On pages 8 and 9 of *The Earth Dragon Awakes,* what is at the center of the Earth? How is the Earth's surface described? What are the names of the two plates under San Francisco? Reread if necessary. *The Earth has a molten core, and it has a "piecrust" with plates on it. San Francisco is on top of the edge of the North American Plate and the Pacific Plate.*

4. What is the name of the fault, and how long and wide is it? *The fault is the San Andreas Fault. It is 650 miles long and 10 miles wide in parts.*

5. Compare Henry and Chin, using a Venn diagram found in Student Folder (Venn Diagram: Chin vs. Henry, figure B.15 in Appendix B). How are their lives similar, and how are they different? Consider their ethnicities, where they live, schools, homes, interests, and social status.

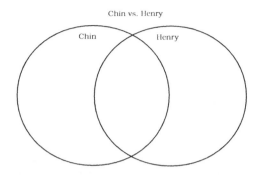

Sample answers:

Chin	Both	Henry
Lived in America for 2 years		Always lived in America
Poor		Wealthy
	Both live in San Francisco	
	Both like the same books – penny dreadfuls!	
Attends a Chinese school in Chinatown		Attends an American school
	Both want to be different from their dads	
	Both are only children	
Learning English		Teaching English to Chin
Speaks Chinese at home		Speaks English at home
Son of servant		Son of family who hires servant
Lives in crowded Chinatown		Lives in a wealthy area
	Both are about same age (9 and 8)	
	Both have busy fathers	

6. What do Henry and Chin seem to think about their dads? Who is Chin's hero? *Both do not want to be like their busy fathers. Chin's hero is Marshall Earp.*

7. Add Chin and his father Ah Sing (on one line together) to your How We Came Tracker, table A.14.

Add to Timeline

- Date, time, and estimated magnitude of the San Francisco Earthquake: *5:11 AM, April 18, 1906, magnitude 8.25*

9.1.2 Historical Places: Chinatown, SF

Big Question: What makes a place a place?

1. From your knowledge of Chinatown from *The Earth Dragon Awakes*, describe Chinatown. *crowded, lots of people playing games and music, tenement homes*

2. What activities go on around Chin's house? *mahjong games and fiddle playing*

3. How do Chin and his dad get around? *cable car*

4. How many people live in Chinatown? *10,000 people*

5. What languages do people speak? *many Chinese dialects*

Read to Students To give you more of an idea of a Chinese immigrant experience in San Francisco, read "In the New Garden," in *California Out of the Box Supplement*, page 15 (*Stories from Where We Live*, page 139).

6. What is the "New Garden?" *a term used by the Chinese in the 1900s to describe Golden Gate Park*

7. In this poem, what imagery does the poet use in describing Golden Gate Park? *willow and peach trees, grass, a pathway, blooming flowers*

8. How does this immigrant see his new homeland? *There are many things for him to enjoy; he'd like to relax and enjoy his experience in the garden all over again.*

9. Use Google Images to view some photos of Golden Gate Park and Chinatown. Google search terms: photos historic san francisco chinatown and photos golden gate park

9.1.3   Pages 19-32

Big Question: How do living things survive in a changing environment? (Murdoch, 2015)

1. After the earthquake, whose house is worse, Henry's or Chin's? Are they able to get out? How do their family members fare?
Chin's house is worse, as the ground floor collapses on him and his dad and they are buried alive. Henry is trapped in his room, but no walls have fallen. His mom and dad are okay.

2. What noises and other things do they observe around them in the city after the quake? How do Henry's neighbors fare? How do the animals respond? *The cable car tracks are in strange shapes and homes are sitting at odd angles. Pipes are gushing in the street. The street is split open. The house of one of their neighbors has fallen and the family is trapped. Horse and cattle are running through the streets.*

3. What is happening under the streets after the quake? What is caused by the water that is thrown under the streets? *The city sits on a landfill, and as water is tossed under the surface, it mixes with the landfill. It causes liquefaction, which means the ground becomes like quicksand.*

9.1.4 Pages 33-39

Big Question: Does any good come from disasters?

1. How do Chin and his dad eventually get themselves out? *Chin starts to dig himself and his father out. Ah Quon sees them and helps dig them out also.*

2. What are some ways Mr. Travis helps his neighbors? *Mr. Travis helps to rescue two other families. He even gives money to pay a surrey driver to take one of his neighbors to the hospital.*

Refection In your opinion, is this disaster bringing out the worst in people or the best in people? *The community in San Francisco is working hard to help rescue each other. When they put together a water brigade, Mrs. Travis comments that it is bringing out the best in people.*

Reflection Remember a time when something difficult brought out the best in someone you know. What was the story? Can you remember a story about when disaster brought about the worst in someone?

9.1.5 Pages 40-56

Big Question: How are the earth, humans, and animals connected?

1. Name some ways the aftershocks are impacting the survivor's plans. What are people doing to cope? What choices are people making about their homes and belongings?
The aftershocks are making weakened buildings fall and they are starting fires. People are throwing their belongings out of their windows to get out fast, in some cases injuring or seriously harming others. Many people are moving all of their furniture outside.

2. How is the community working together to fight the fire? *They start a bucket brigade.*

3. How are the animals reacting to the chaos? *Animals, such as a bull and horses, are bolting away and running through the streets.*

4. What sources of water are the firemen tapping? *The firemen are drawing water from underground cisterns and pumping salt water from the bay.*

9.2   Week 25

9.2.1   Pages 57-72

Big Question: What makes a hero? (Murdoch, 2015)

1. Once they are freed from their home, how do Ah Sing and Chin make money? *In exchange for money, Ah Sing and his "partner" Chin help a merchant load a wagon with the merchant's goods.*

2. What does Chin decide about his father, and why is it hard for him to "sit there and do nothing" when he is injured? *Chin realizes his father is brave. Ah Quon tells him it took a lot of courage for his father to come to California. His father simply cannot sit and do nothing.*

3. How are people trying to escape the city and the fires? *People escape the city on dangerously overloaded boats.*

4. How are people deciding to rescue their belongings? *They put their belongings on blankets, in wagons, on lawnmowers, and in cribs. Mrs. Travis uses an umbrella to keep the embers off her.*

5. Look at Google Images for some photos of the 1906 San Francisco earthquake. Google search terms: 1906 san francisco photos

9.2.2   A Closer Look: Using Figurative Language

Teacher's Note   This section highlights the use of simile and personification. (See "Poetry: Reading & Project," page 25 for previous discussion of figurative language.) These two language tools are powerful to enable students to describe difficult situations. If students can come up with pictures about how they feel, this skill may help them bravely look at their feelings in a given moment.

Big Question: How do we explain our feelings?

Simile Warm-Up   Brainstorm some examples of one thing that can be said to be like another. Read the following sentences to students and have them come up with their own words to replace italicized words:

- fast squirrel: ran like a (*puma*) to get away from the large dog

- bright red car: drove as fast as an (*Olympic runner*) to get away from the police car

- The (*100 year old dilapidated shed*): fell over like a tower of bricks

- the (*child's new airplane drone*): soared over the city like a hawk over a mountain range

Read to Students and Discuss   The author says the "fire is like a monster," and the earthquake is like "the earth dragon that is looking for its last meal."

1. In what ways is the fire behaving like an "earth dragon?" What are some physical things this "earth dragon" has done?
   The fire is spreading like a dragon that picks its next meal, the dragon fire combines forces with its brother and sisters to make a huge fire, it has destroyed houses, it has burnt up the town.

2. Think of a difficult situation you have experienced. It could be anything – a problem with a friend, feeling overwhelmed, being angry about something, moving or changing schools when you didn't want to, etc.

3. Come up with a few similes to describe that "bad thing." How did that situation feel? List them in your Composition Book.

   Some examples:

   - *tidal wave/tsunami: Food poisoning came over me like a tsunami.*
   - *raging storm: The fight with my friend was like a raging storm.*

- *lightening strike: The car rounded the corner as fast as a lightening strike.*

- *climbing a mountain: Studying for the test felt like climbing a huge mountain.*

4. Pick one simile from the last question and demonstrate it, imbuing it with the emotional qualities of the image or situation. Some ways to show it are in a drawing, poem, writing piece, or sculpture.

Example: When I was in second grade and my aunt and uncle got divorced, I found out I would not get to see my favorite cousin anymore. My cousin and my aunt were already moving out of state.

In that situation, I felt like a piece of paper that was being torn in half. My friendship felt ripped in two as I was separated from a good childhood friend. To demonstarte this simile, I could make a collage with paper torn in two.

9.2.3   Pages 73-95

Big Question: How safe is our community? (Murdoch, 2015)

1. What new strategy, involving dynamite, are the firefighters using to hold back the fires? Describe how this strategy works. *Instead of letting the fire burn the buildings, one by one, using dynamite they destroy the buildings first to diminish the fire source, hoping to slow the fire down.*

2. When the Travises finally escape the area of their home, they go to a large field area. What types of ethnicities do they find at this field? *Germans, Mexicans, and Italians*

3. Eventually, the 3 smaller fires grow into a Great Fire. This fire creates strong winds. What forces cause the winds to erupt? What makes this fire so dangerous?
The Great Fire causes warm air to rise, and cool air pushes in. Cold air being pushed in caused winds that could even pull people in. Because the fire was extremely hot – 2,000 degrees celcius – any fire source like wood or flesh would instantly burn if it was close to the fire.

4. Once people flee the city, where are some places they are forced to relocate to? How do white people see the Chinese? Why are the Chinese forced to live separately? *50,000 people left San Francisco; the Navy brought many to Oakland, where many were living in tents. White Americans did not want to live near the Chinese, so the Chinese were forced to live in special camps.*

5. How does the rescue situation unfold for Chin and Ah Sing and the Travises? How are they able to work together? *Chin and Ah Sing have gone to a cousin's fish warehouse in Oakland. They see the Travises in a crowd that has fled there. Chin asks his cousin Ah Bing if they can stay at the warehouse, and he agrees.*

9.2.4 Pages 96-105

Big Question: What types of disasters change people's housing?

1. Three days after the earthquake, the fire finally dies down. In the process, some drastic measures are taken. Name a few ways the townspeople and the firemen have fought the fire. What extraordinary measures have they taken?
   People soak curtains in water and wine to stop the fire; in bucket brigades, all buckets, including milk bottles, are used; when fires start burning roof shingles, firemen cut the burning sections off roofs; doors are used by firemen as shields against the fire.

2. Where do the Travises decide they will stay during the rebuilding phase? What options are open to Chinese families? *The Travises decide to set up a tent in Golden Gate Park during the rebuilding phase. The Chinese are not allowed in the park, so they must live in Oakland during rebuilding.*

3. How do the Travises and Chin and his father decide they will rebuild their lives? *The Travises will rebuild their home. Chin and his father want to return to Chinatown and work for the Travises. Chin will return to Chinese school.*

4. How have Chin's and Henry's ideas changed about what a hero is? What do they think it means to be a true hero? What ways have

their fathers modeled being a hero to them? *Chin and Henry see their fathers as heroes now. Their fathers have been heroes by being brave during the earthquake and fire.*

9.2.5 Afterword

Teacher's Note For more on the Angel Island Immigration Station, check our website: `http://carriershellcurriculum.com/` for an art/poetry lesson plan download.

 Big Question: How and why do we remember/commemorate events of the past? (Murdoch, 2015)

1. Where were most Chinese sent to live during the rebuilding phase? *Most lived in Oakland.*

2. Describe the controversy about how to rebuild Chinatown. Where was it finally rebuilt? *People wanted the Chinese to give up their prime land and take less desirable land. The white landowners in Chinatown also wanted their renters back, so it was decided to rebuild Chinatown in the same place.*

3. How has the author's life been reflected in elements of this story? In what ways has his family's story been similar? At what island did many Chinese immigrants stop at near San Francisco? *The author's grandfather was a houseboy – like Chin and Ah Sing. He came to Angel Island the day after the earthquake. His father also came in through Angel Island Immigration Station.*

4. What does the city of San Francisco do on April 18 each year to remember the earthquake? *A fire hydrant at 20th and Church gets a new coat of paint.*

5. How big was the 1906 earthquake now thought to be? *between 7.7 and 7.9 on the Richter scale*

9.3 Week 26

9.3.1 Earth Science: Layers of the Earth

> **Teacher's Note** This section begins the discussion of the science behind earthquakes. For these sections, you may check out a library reference book on the Earth such as the ones listed in the unit supply list, or look up the information online.

Big Question: Is nature organized or disorganized?

1. Using Google Images or a library reference book, look up some pictures of a diagram of the Earth. Then fill in the Layers of the Earth Diagram (figure B.16 in Appendix B), identifying the inner core (solid), outer core (liquid), mantle, and the crust (oceanic and continental). The key is provided below. **Google search terms: layers of earth diagram**

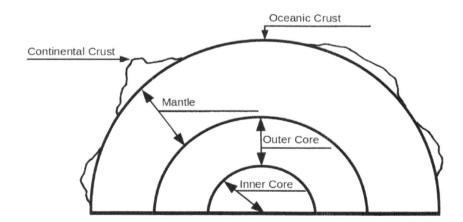

2. Use Google Images to look at a topographical (or satellite) map showing the San Andreas Fault. **Topographical maps** show height dimension in landforms, such as the height of the mountains and the depths of the valleys. **Google search terms: topographical map david lynch san andreas fault.** (The best map should have an ivory background. Link provided below.)

   `https://geology.com/articles/san-andreas-fault.shtml`

3. Using the map in the link above, what compass directions does the San Andreas Fault line travel across California? What landforms are on either side of the fault (i.e., ocean, valleys, mountains)? Which directions are the plates moving? *The fault runs north to south. On either side of the San Andreas are mountains. The east side of the fault is moving south, and the west side of the fault is moving north.*

4. On your California Map (figure B.2), trace the line of the San Andreas Fault. Label it and place arrows showing which direction the plates are moving.

   Review What are the names of these two plates? Label these on your California Map next to the fault. **Google search terms: california tectonic plates** *the Pacific and the North American Plates*

5. Look at Google Images for some photos of the San Andreas fault. There are some fairly dramatic ones! **Google search terms: san andreas fault photos**

9.3.2 Geology: More on Tectonic Plates

Read "Ocean and Coastal Topography" in *Audubon*, pages 14-15.

Big Question: How are landforms shaped? (Murdoch, 2015)

1. What is slowly happening to the California coastline? *It is erroding, or becoming part of the ocean.*

2. What is happening to the San Francisco Bay? *It is slowly filling with mud from the Sacramento River. Without dredging, it will be filled in a few thousand years.*

Read "Tectonic Origins," in *Audubon*, pages 16-17.

3. From your reading, what type of a fault line is the San Andreas fault, and why do you think this? *The San Andreas is a transform fault, as the two sides are sliding laterally past each other.*

4. What are the 2 other fault line boundaries, and which ways do they move? *The two other boundaries are the divergent (plates move apart), and the convergent boundary (plates collide, buckle, and make mountains).*

5. **Plate Movement Model Project:** Using two handtowels placed next to each other (your plates!), show how a transform fault, a divergent fault, and a convergent fault impact each other as they move. Which fault is the most dramatic? Project source: Carmela Gomes, interview by Christine Echeverri, Pasadena, July 3, 2018.

6. Look briefly at a map of the major global tectonic plates on Google Images. List the names of the 9 largest plates on Earth's Major Tectonic Plates Table (table A.24). Google search terms: earth tectonic plates map

	Plate
1	*North American Plate*
2	*Pacific Plate*
3	*African Plate*
4	*South American Plate*
5	*Eurasian Plate*
6	*Australian Plate*
7	*Antarctic Plate*
8	*Will vary* - Indian Plate*
9	*Will vary* - Nazca Plate*

* For the last two plates, students could also include Philippine, Cocos, Arabian, Scotia, Juan de Fuca, or Caribbean Plate.

Writing   Looking back on the diagram on the layers of the Earth, plates, and the San Andreas Fault, have students write 1 paragraph with 5-7 sentences about what they have learned about plate tectonics in their Composition Books.

Also, have students write 1-2 questions they have about the plates.

Sample paragraph: The main fault under California is the San Andreas Fault. It is 650 miles long and 10 miles wide in some places. It is a transform fault, which is formed where the two plates – the North American and the Pacific Plates – slide past each other.

There are 4 layers of the Earth – the inner core, outer core, mantle, and crust. The crust involves both ocean and continental portions.

There are 7 major plates and 8 minor ones. They mostly share the names of the continents.

Student questions: These will vary. If students seem particularly engaged, give extra research time for finding the answers.

Bonus   Using *Audubon* (page 16), describe how the Sierra Nevadas and the Central Valley were formed. (Students will go to the Central Valley in the last book of the curriculum, *Esperanza Rising*.) What is the name of the plate that was pushed under the North American continent?

As the Farallon Plate pushed under the North American Plate/continent, this caused the coastal mountains to form. Later, as the plate got pushed even lower under the continent, magma was liquefied and forced upwards which formed the granites of the Sierra Nevada. Visit this NASA website below for a visualization of this process:
`https://svs.gsfc.nasa.gov/1322`

9.3.3   Geology: Rocks & Minerals Overview

Read   about Vasquez Rocks. Link listed in *California Out of the Box Supplement*. ["Vasquez Rocks" poem mentioned below found in *Stories from*

Where We Live, page 106.]

    Big Question: Where is the past in the present? (Murdoch, 2015)

1. What trees, plants, and animals are found here? *lizards, jackrabbits, manzanita, and juniper trees*

 Look at Google Images for photos of the rocks. **Google search terms: vasquez rocks photos**

2. What major city are these rocks close to? *Los Angeles*

3. What type of habitat are these rocks situated in? (You will come back to this habitat in your last book!) *desert*

4. Here is a short video that gives more information about the park (*Vasquez Rocks: Film Locations and Hiking* on California Through My Lens site):

 `http://californiathroughmylens.com/vasquez-rocks.`

5. From the "Vasquez Rocks" poem, what people groups have their history intertwined with the rocks? *Shoshone Indians, Spaniards, bandits like Tiburcio Vasquez*

 Bonus Who are these "Ghosts of Vasquez" from the poem? Spend some time looking into the stories of Tiburcio Vasquez and other famous people and films that have been filmed here.

 This site gives an excellent history of the rocks (Santa Clarita Valley TV):

 `http://www.scvhistory.com/scvhistory/vasquez011574glenn.htm.`

Read "Minerals and Natural Resources" and "Rocks," in *Audubon*, pages 26-30.

6. From "The Rock Cycle," on page 29: What are the three basic classes of rocks?

   - *Igneous rocks*
   - *Sedimentary rocks*
   - *Metamorphic rocks*

7. Looking at the diagram on page 29, describe how the rock cycle works.

   Igneous rocks solidify near the Earth's surface from molten lava flows. Over time these rocks erode and force sediment down, which forms sedimentary rock, as layers upon layers are deposited. Through heating and cooling, sedimentary rock metamorphs, or changes, to become metamorphic rock. Then, through geothermal heat, the metamorphic rock becomes molten and shoots back up to the Earth's surface to become igneous rock, thus repeating the cycle.

8. Which of these 3 types of rocks describe Vasquez Rocks? *Vasquez rocks are a combination of igneous and sedimentary rocks.*

9. Do you have a favorite rock or mineral? Which is your favorite mentioned in the *Audubon* guide? Which of the 3 types of rocks is your favorite?

Review Based on your reading from the *Audubon* guide, which of the three types of rock is gold, and why? *Gold is metamorphic rock, as it has been transformed through heating and cooling.*

9.4   Week 27

9.4.1   Geology: Rock Tests

> **Teacher's Note** Have students pick one test to perform. If time permits, try both!

Big Question: What are rocks made of?

Test A: Rock Hardness

Have students look at the Mohs Hardness Scale in Student Folder, table A.25.

Read to Students As the *Audubon* guide points out, merely looking at the color of minerals is not the best way to identify them. A truer way of categorizing them to is to perform different tests on them to see how they react under pressure.

One of the most important tests is the Mohs Hardness Test. In this test, minerals have been generally categorized as to their hardness.

Mohs Hardness Scale

Mineral	Hardness
Talc	1
Gypsum	2
Calcite	3
Flourite	4
Apatite	5
Orthoclase	6
Quartz	7
Topaz	8
Corundum	9
Diamond	10

Source: Steven Schimmrich, "Mohs Scale of Hardness," *Hudson Valley Geologist,* August 31, 2010, accessed July 12, 2018, http://hudsonvalleygeologist.blogspot.com/2010/08/mohs-scale-of-hardness.html.

Looking at this chart, is talcum powder harder than a diamond? *No, a diamond is the hardest mineral.*

Mohs Hardness Test

Supplies:

- Gardening gloves

- Safety goggles

- Sharpie marker

- Masking tape

- Steel file

- Quartz rock

- 5-8 Rocks

1. To do this test, students should choose/find 5-8 rocks. With tape and a Sharpie, students should number each rock beginning with #1. It is best if students choose rocks that are not expensive ones bought from a museum.

2. **Safety Note** - Work outside, in an area where students have plenty of light. Students should not do this test on expensive furniture, and should always make marks away from the body. For protection, students should wear gardening gloves and safety goggles.

3. With a quartz rock, make one long deep groove in sample #1. The mark needs to be made in one determined, hard motion. If students do not have quartz, a pure steel file will do. It has a hardness of about 6.5.

4. After students make this mark, students should look to see if a groove was made. If the mark rubs off, it is "mineral powder" and not a real mark. If a groove mark was made, then the "marking material" was harder than sample #1. If the marking material was scratched, sample #1 was harder. If both of them are marked, or are difficult to make marks on, their hardness is near equivalent.

5. Students should fill in the following chart in their Student Folders, table A.26:

Sample #	Estimated Hardness	Rock type: Igneous, Sedimentary, or Metamorphic	Notes
1			
2			
3			
4			
5			
6			
7			
8			

6. For more information on this test, visit:

`http://geology.com/minerals/mohs-hardness-scale.shtml`

Test B: Fracture/Cleavage

Read to Students Another test that can reveal the type of mineral a sample is – the fracture/cleavage test.

Materials needed:

- Safety goggles

- Masking tape

- Sharpie marker

- Hammer

- 5-8 Rocks

- Old towel (for work surface)

Important: Wear safety googles for all tests, as sharp bits of rock can fly off when struck. **Everyone present should wear goggles**; rocks can fly off unpredictably and can hit an eye at any moment when struck with a hammer.

1. Choose 5-8 samples of different sizes and textures. With tape and a marker, label each rock starting with #1. Again, students shouldn't use prized rocks from a collection.

2. In an outside location, put on safety goggles. Students should place on an old towel on a table or on the ground. With a hammer, hit the rock and notice how it breaks apart. Does it crumble, flake off in sheets, or break along any flat planes? If it flakes off, it is said to have cleavage. If the sample crumbles irregularly, it is said to fracture. Some rocks have both multiple directions of cleavage, and fracture along non-cleavage sides. If any side breaks along a flat plane, it has cleavage in *that* direction. Some rock samples might have *both* fracture and cleavage. This test can reveal interesting observations about rocks, and will help give students more of an idea of a rock's crystalline make-up than might otherwise be noticeable in only viewing the rock.

3. Look at the following website to explore the types of cleavage; it can be along one plane or several.

   `http://academic.brooklyn.cuny.edu`
   `/geology/grocha/mineral/cleavage.html`

4. Have students fill in table A.27 and make notes on the fracture or cleavage of each sample.

Sample #	Fracture, Cleavage, or Both	Rock Type: Igneous, Sedimentary, or Metamorphic	Notes
1			
2			
3			
4			
5			
6			
7			
8			

9.4.2 Geological Research: California's Major Quakes

Big Question: Does learning about past events help us in the present?

Read to Students You will spend some time researching the largest California quakes since the 1800s.

Look at: `http://www.conservation.ca.gov/index/Earthquakes/Pages/ca-big-quakes.aspx`

or the US Geological Survey for California.

Google search terms: california largest earthquakes since 1800

Have students fill in table A.28 in their Student Folders. Enter quakes with the highest magnitude first. Answers below are from the Conservation website (link above), but may vary depending on data source used.

Largest California Earthquakes (1800-Present)

	Date	Magnitude	Location	Number of People Killed
1	*Jan. 9, 1857*	*7.9*	*Fort Tejon*	*2*
2	*April 18, 1906*	*7.9*	*San Francisco*	*3,000*
3	*March 26, 1872*	*7.8*	*Owens Valley*	*27*
4	*July 21, 1952*	*7.5*	*Kern County*	*12*
5	*January 31, 1922*	*7.3*	*West of Eureka*	*0*
6	*Nov. 4, 1927*	*7.3*	*SW of Lompoc*	*0*
7	*June 28, 1992*	*7.3*	*Landers*	*1*
8	*January 22, 1923*	*7.2*	*Mendocino*	*0*

Discussion Have students use crayons or colored pencils. Look at the chart and answer the following questions:

1. Which earthquake had the largest magnitude? Color it red. *Fort Tejon*

2. Which earthquake had the smallest magnitude? Color it pink. *Mendocino*

3. Which earthquake happened the furthest back in time? Color it purple. *Fort Tejon*

4. Which of these earthquakes was the most recent? Color it blue. *Landers*

5. Find out which of these earthquakes occurred closest to your home. Color it brown. *Answers will vary.*

6. Which earthquake caused the most deaths? Color it yellow. *San Francisco*

7. Which earthquakes had the fewest casualties? Color them orange. *Eureka, Lompoc, Mendocino*

Earthquake Safety Project   Safety is an important fact to focus on while looking at earthquakes. While earthquakes cannot be prevented, there are things one can do to be safer in case one should strike. The `Ca.gov` site has good resources for families as well as lists of supplies to include in an emergency kit. A relevant application to earthquake safety is to make a family emergency kit. Students can write up or print out a list of supplies, see what their family already has, and then procure items.

What to do in case of an earthquake: `http://www.conservation.ca.gov/index/Earthquakes/Pages/qh_earthquakes_what.aspx`

`https://www.cdph.ca.gov/Programs/EPO/Pages/BI_Natural-Disasters_Earthquakes.aspx`

Preparing an Emergency Kit: `https://www.cdph.ca.gov/Programs/EPO/Pages/PrepareanEmergencySupplyKit.aspx`

9.4.3   Habitat Study: Marsh & Wetlands

Read to Students   Much of the area around San Francisco is rich in the salt marsh/wetlands habitat. Looking at the California maps in the front and back of the *Audubon* guide, can you guess why? *A number of rivers, such as the Sacramento and San Joaquin Rivers, flow into it.*

Read   "The Marsh at the Edge of Arcata" in *The California Coast* reader (*Stories from Where We Live*), beginning on page 109.

Big Question: What resources can be reused?

1. What are some of the animals you hear about in this story? What are some of the plants that are mentioned? *Animals include: red-tailed hawk, snowy egret, mallard ducks, great blue heron, marsh wrens, black-crowned night heron, and kites. Plants include: fennel, pickleweed, bulrush, cattails, duckweed, and cordgrass.*

2. How has this city decided to process its waste water? What might have prompted them to try this? What did they initially try, and how did that impact the area? What is the process now for filtering the water? *Arcata processes its wastewater by sending it through various filters and then several ponds where plants remove harmful pollutants. Initially they sent the harmful toxic water straight to the ocean. Then the city treated the water with chlorine, which cleaned the water, but poisoned plants and animals.*

3. What is an estuary? *An estuary is a natural area where fresh water mixes with salt water. Inland streams that flow to the ocean water create estuary environments.*

4. Using Google Maps or the *Audubon* guide (page 379), locate the city of Arcata and label it on your California Map, figure B.2.

5. Use Google Images to look at some pictures of Arcata Marsh. What types of plants and animals do you see? Google search terms: arcata marsh photos
There are winding waterways with cattails in between. There are hawks and ducks.

Read   "Rivers, Lakes, and Wetlands" in *Audubon* on pages 48-49 and "Salt Marshes" in *The California Coast* reader (*Stories from Where We Live*), on page 214.

6. Where is the largest salt marsh in California located? *San Francisco Bay*

7. What main challenge do plants face living in a salt marsh environment? *Plants must be able to process salt.*

8. Use Google Images to look up photos of marshes and wetlands in California. Google search terms: california salt marsh estuary photos

9. Fill in Habitat Tracker B in Student Folder for marshes. On your Habitat Description sheet, draw a picture of the land, a plant, and an animal, and label them. Write a short paragraph about this habitat (or you may substitute with the Native Habitat Home Building Project).

Habitat	Trees/Shrubs	Flowering Plants	Animals	Location (cities)
Salt Marsh	*Eelgrass, pickleweed, cordgrass*	*Cattails*	*Avocets, bay ghost shrimp, harvest mice, ospreys, egrets*	*San Francisco, Arcata, Baywood/Los Osos*

Sample habitat description: Salt marshes are rich areas found on the coast where freshwater mixes with salt water. Many birds are found in this habitat such as osprey, egrets, herons, and ducks. The main plants are eelgrass, pickleweed, and cordgrass – all plants in this area have adapted to process salt. This area is also rich in mollusks and crustaceans like shrimp.

9.4.4   Natural Resource: Water

Teacher's Note   This section will take a brief look at a much needed resource within California – water!

Big Question: Why is water important?

Review & Discuss

- What natural resource was most needed to fight the fires in San Francisco? *water*

- What might a city do if they run out of water during such a disaster? *Find a new source.*

- How do cities located in drier climates get water? Explore:

  `https://www.watereducation.org/topic-hetch-hetchy`

  to find out more information about the Hetch Hetchy water project. Under "Aquapedia Background" you will find detailed information about this water project.

  Bonus   Do you remember who fought against the Hetch Hetchy reservior? *John Muir*

- What area does the dam provide water for? *San Francisco area*

- How many water and dam projects do you see listed under the "Dams, Reservoirs, and Water Projects" tab? *12*

- Choose 1-2 other water projects to read more about. For each project, find out the following (list also appears in Student Folder in table A.29):

  - Note where the dam or water storage area is located.

  - Where does the water originate, and where does it go?

  - What areas or cities are serviced by the water?

  - Which one of the major cities that you initially labeled on your California Map does the water flow to (i.e.; San Francisco, Los Angeles, Sacramento, Monterey, Santa Barbara, San Diego)?

  - Do you imagine the cities that benefit from this water project would grow as big as they have without this project?

  - Any other interesting facts.

- Haves students write up a paragraph in Composition Books on each water project they explore.

Sample paragraph: The 444-mile California Aqueduct brings water from Oroville Dam to Los Angeles, and eventually Lake Perris in Southern California. It parallels the 5 freeway through the San Joaquin Valley.

Los Angeles would not have grown as much as it has without this water. The Los Angeles River does not provide enough water for residents of this city.

Bonus Looking at the map of California and precipitation you printed out from a "Weather: San Francisco & Beyond," begining on page 149, note where the top of the water project you researched is located. Is it in a valley or in the mountains? *The Oroville Dam is located 70 miles north of Sacramento by the Feather River. It is located in the foothills of the Sierras.*

Add to Timeline

- Decade Hetch Hetchy Dam was built *1920s*

Bonus Project: Water Scarcity Research Look online, in the *Los Angeles Times* or other California newspaper, and find a recent article about water scarcity. Google search terms: california water scarcity articles

Discuss the article. Answer the following as they apply:

1. What cities are involved?

2. Why are they water challenged?

3. How long has the area been in this situation?

4. What are the major threats to the water supply?

5. What measures is the city implementing to help with the water crisis?

6. What should rainfall level have been?

7. What level is it at currently?

9.5   Week 28

9.5.1   Research: Internet vs. Books

Teacher's Note   How reliable is the Internet for research? Students today seem very comfortable "googling" it. But what is the value of the information they find? This brief foray into comparing the Internet with other resources is important to discuss. Either read or put the following information in your own words for your students:

"It is very important to know that just because some information is presented on the Internet, this does not make it true. It is relatively easy for a person to post information online. Because of this, books and printed material are actually more thoroughly reviewed. They have had teams poring over each word and checking the accuracy of the information. It costs a lot more money to write and print a book than to add to a `Wikipedia` article or start a blog!

The Internet functions well as a starting point for your work. For formal writing, be sure to go to the library and check out books."

Big Question: How do we know if something is true? (Murdoch, 2015)

Notetaking

Read to Students   In general, when you do research, you should take notes on what you read; you can place these notes in your Composition Book. You should not copy word for word what another writer has already written. You should also note the name of the book and author, and the date you took the note and the page number; make specific notes next to the page number with the information you would like to remember.

For Internet research, you should *not* literally copy and paste words from a site into a document or into your report. Make a print out of the article that has the site title, link, and the date. Highlight the information you found interesting in the article with a highlighter marker.

Research Mash-Up: Internet vs. Books

1. Choose 1 topic or animal from the *Audubon* guide.

2. Read about it in *Audubon*.

3. Type the topic name into a search engine. Find an online article on this subject and print it out.

4. At the library or on your book shelves, find another source on this same topic.

5. Read each of your sources and take notes. Highlight your printed Internet article. Complete table A.30 in Student Folder.

Discuss What did you learn that was different in each of the sources? Which one was easiest to use?

Discuss Which source did you like best, and why?

Sample Topic: Monarch Butterfly

Audubon Guide	Internet	Library Book
Pages: *215*	Website: *Wikipedia: Monarch Butterfly*	Book Title/Author: *Monarchs and Milkweed, by Anurag Agrawal*
	Date: *April 11, 2018*	Pages: *All*
Notes: *Orange butterfly with black wings, male has a dot on wing, migrates south in winter, eats milkweed*	Notes: *Monarchs west of the Rockies often migrate to southern California; larvae only eat milkweed; adults eat lots of types of nectar.*	Notes: *Monarch butterflies eat milkweed, which is a poisonous plant. They have 4 generations that live in their native location, and then the 5th generation migrates. The cycle continues.*

9.5.2   End of Unit IV Questions

Questions for further consideration:

1. What do you wonder? What can you do about it?

2. Imagine you are a person of Chinese descent in San Francisco. You live in Chinatown, and you and your family work hard. After the earthquake, you see people of Caucasian descent come back to live and rebuild, but you are not allowed back. How might you feel? Write a journal entry from Chin's perspective. What might he hope for? What might he miss about his old home of Chinatown (or in China)?

3. Chin has come from China to be with his father in a new country to help out at an American family's home. María Rosalia, from *Valley of the Moon*, though half Native American and half white, lives with a Spanish family. Both are "home," but "not home." They are not living in their original cultural home with both parents. In what ways might Chin and María Rosalia feel similarly? Reflect on a time when you felt not quite in your element, where you felt out of place in a group of people. How did you "find your place"? What advice do you have for a friend who might be in a similar situation. Write a "Dear Abby" letter explaining the problem and a response.

   Similarities: María Rosalia and Chin might both feel that they would like to pursue their interests instead of working so hard for another family. They both read a lot. Both are learning English. They might both miss their mothers.

4. Time has passed from Karana's years alone on San Nicolas Island to the days of Chin and Henry Travis in San Francisco. Imagine if Henry or Chin picked up a copy of the *Island of the Blue Dolphins*. How might Henry or Chin describe their life to Karana? What advice might they give her about living in a city – and the fun things and challenges of living there? Write a letter from Henry or Chin to Karana about how she could survive in a city environment.

   They might tell her about the cable cars and the penny dreadfuls they read. They might tell her about their experiences going to school. They could discuss how they live – Henry in a home and Chin in a tenement building. They could tell her how they get food by going to markets. They could tell her she wouldn't need to spend so much time hunting and making weapons as there are police to protect them and markets to buy food where they live.

5. You have now covered 5 habitats in California. Review your Habitat Tracker Charts. Which one is your favorite, and why? What do you like most about that place?

6. What is your favorite rock or mineral? Choose a mineral that is found in the state of California from *Audubon* and research it. Where is it found? Which of the three classes of rocks is it? Write 1-3 paragraphs about your findings. Also, using simile, compose a poem about your rock. (What colors and/or materials could it be compared to?) Finally, either draw or take a photo of your rock.

7. Make a family earthquake kit and put together an emergency plan. Who will do what jobs? Where will you meet each other? See "Geological Research: California's Major Quakes," page 179 for sites and resources related to earthquake preparation.

Unit V

Esperanza

(Hope)

Hope Amidst Great Depression

Chapter 10

Unit Introduction

10.1 Supplies for This Unit

1. Resources used throughout

   - See list on page 2

2. Section 10.2.3: Biology: The Monarch

   - Library reference book on monarch butterfly, page 197

3. Section 10.2.4: Introduction to Unit V Projects

   - Various materials depending on chosen project, page 199

4. Chapter 11: *Esperanza Rising*

   - *Esperanza Rising* (Pam Muñoz Ryan, ISBN 978-0-439-12042-5)
   - Library book with version of the Myth of the Phoenix for "*Los Higos*, pages 39-57" chapter, page 213
   - Voice recorder (phone app or cassette tape for "Research: Oral History," page 230)
   - Index cards: 8x5 and 3x5 or 4x6
   - Markers, crayons, or colored pencils
   - Sharpie marker
   - Ribbon or string

- 24" stick from yard/home/hike
- Tape or glue
- Glue gun
- Banner paper (6" wide recommended)
- Optional: materials for "Cutting Potato Eyes" bonus activity, section 11.3.4, page 222
- Optional: materials for Native Habitat Home Design, page 18

10.2 Week 29

10.2.1 Review: The Story of California

Teacher's Note This section is a brief review of the curriculum. Spend 15-20 minutes with students in a review discussion. Students should have their Student Folders handy.

How We Came

People have come to California in many different ways.

Big Question: What stands out about stories you've heard so far?

1. Looking at your How We Came Tracker (table A.14), which of the characters had the longest voyage in terms of distance? *Junípero Serra, Jack or Praiseworthy, or Cut-Eye Higgins*

2. Who had the toughest voyage? *Walter and Nelly Johnston or Junípero Serra*

3. Who had the shorter voyages? *Karana and María Rosalia*

4. Which migration journey would you want to make?

Timeline

Have students lay out timeline index cards in chronological order (or print out Timetoast timeline) and answer the following questions:

Big Question: How do humans change over time? (Murdoch, 2015)

1. When does the timeline start? *4.6 billion years ago with the Earth's formation*

2. What is the most recent point? *The most recent point would be the date from student's memory in "Poetry Reflection: Time," page 38.*

3. What is your favorite moment?

California Map

Have students look at their California Maps (figure B.2).

Big Question: How are maps and history related?

1. Have students locate where they live.

2. What area might you want to visit now, and why?

Habitats

Students should locate their Habitat Tracker A, and Habitat Tracker B, and Habitat Description Sheets.

Big Question: How does where we live affect HOW we live? (Murdoch, 2015)

1. Which habitat is your favorite, and why?

2. What are some places or parks you could go to observe that habitat?

3. If students did the Native Habitat Home Building Project, which house is their favorite, and why?

Your Favorite Things

Big Question: How do you know what you like?

After reviewing these 4 aspects to the story of California, discuss the following:

1. If you were going to explore more about California, what area or time period would you choose?

2. Which events, places, or stories were your favorite?

3. In Composition Books, have students make a list of their favorite five places, events, or stories.

Primary Sources: Newspapers

Teacher's Note   This section explores a historical newspaper archive. If you are running short on time, you can merely introduce students to site. Who knows what type of research they may do in the future?

Big Question: What makes the news and why? (Murdoch, 2015)

Some of the best free primary sources of information about the past are newspapers. Because of their daily coverage, they help to fill out how life was experienced in the past. Fortunately, with the Internet there are excellent free sources of newspapers. The California Digital Newspaper Collection (CDNC) features newspaper articles going back to 1846.

```
https://cdnc.ucr.edu/cgi-bin/cdnc
```

Research Exercise:

1. Look at CDNC to find copies of old newspapers.

2. Search the site for the year 1849 and browse articles on mining. Read one or two.

3. Using the list of your 5 favorite things you generated previously, type a few of these items into the database search bar. What do you find?

4. To zoom in, click on the + button. Some of the articles have been transcribed as well.

5. Read a few articles. Are the articles from recent times or from long ago? Do they include illustrations? What do you learn?

6. Print out a PDF copy of one selection.

10.2.2   Music: African Americans Bring Jazz to California in the 1920s

Big Question: Why do people make music? (Murdoch, 2015)

One people group that has not been explored thus far are African Americans. Before World War II, the population of African Americans in California was less than 1% of the total California population. (Source: Wikipedia, "African Americans in California," accessed August 12, 2018, https://en.wikipedia.org/w/index.php?title=African_Americans_in_California&oldid=847184234).

For a good overview of African American migration to Los Angeles, watch *Once Upon a Time in Early Black Los Angeles* by Lloyd F Reese.

```
https://www.youtube.com/watch?v=Wh_X8OeY8N8
```

1. What streets did many African Americans settle on in Los Angeles? *1st and Central Avenue*

2. What major black philanthropist lived in Los Angeles and now has a memorial in downtown LA? *Biddy Mason*

For the feel of 1920s and 30s music, watch *Central Avenue Breakdown* by Bill Kalmenson on Youtube. Note: Some jazz musicians in this video are photographed smoking cigarettes and sitting with drinks in clubs.

```
https://www.youtube.com/watch?v=mJnmOTiRor4
```

Spend a few minutes browsing California Digital Newspaper Archive to explore other famous African American musicians. Some famous ones are Kid Ory, Jelly Roll Morton, and Lionel Hampton. Print out one article or advertisement and keep it in Student Folder.

California Digital Newspaper Archive Link

```
https://cdnc.ucr.edu/cgi-bin/cdnc
```

Add to Timeline

- Jazz Scene in Los Angeles on Central Ave: *1920-30s*

10.2.3 Biology: The Monarch

Teacher's Note This section introduces biological information about the monarch, which will be combined later with symbolic information about the monarch in a curriculum culmination project.

Big Question: What can humans learn from insects?

Read about the monarch butterfly in *Audubon* (page 215), in the "Insects" section. Additionally, do some brief research on the butterfly by either finding an online article or checking out a book from library. This site has good information:

`http://www.monarch-butterfly.com/`.

Google Search terms: monarch butterfly life cycle migration

1. Draw a picture of the butterfly in your Sketch Book.

2. What is its life cycle? *They have 4 stages of development: egg, the larvae (caterpillar), the pupa (chrysalis), and the adult butterfly.*

3. What do caterpillars eat? *milkweed*

4. What is the physical reason they migrate? *They migrate during fall so as to not perish of cold in the winter.*

5. What are some of the countries/places they move between? Trace their migration pattern on your Monarch Migration Map, figure B.17. *They migrate from the eastern US and middle US to Mexico. West of the Rockies, they migrate to the California coast.*

Answer key:

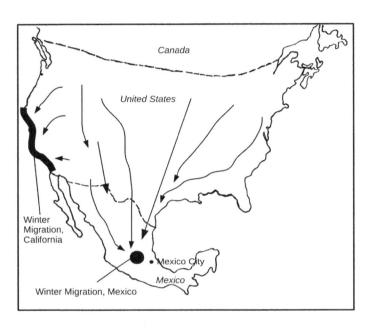

6. Write 1 paragraph in Composition Book about what you have learned about the monarch.

The monarch has 4 stages of development: egg, larvae, pupa, and adult. Every year there are as many as 5 generations; the fifth makes the migration journey. They migrate mostly to Mexico, though the butterflies west of the Rockies migrate to California. The caterpillars eat only milkweed.

10.2.4 Introduction to Unit V Projects

Teacher's Note In this last unit, students will do a more focused overarching project. Reading comprehension questions are provided, but the goal of this unit is to take the story deeper and allow more space for the story to emerge organically. Knowing that it's close to the end of the year, if you or your students are feeling overwhelmed, give yourself permission to drop the questions and focus on the project, or continue with questions and drop the project. It's also okay just to finish the the book and do culminating work after book to wrap up the curriculum.

For an open-ended option, choose option 1.

For 3rd and 4th graders, choose "Botanical Illustration" or "Quiet Action." For 5th-6th graders, the other projects are good candidates.

Additional option: Take a glance at "End of Unit V and End of Curriculum Questions" (page 239) to consider discussion or writing prompts instead of Unit V Projects.

Unit V Projects:

1. From your studies, what has mattered to you? What can you do about it?

2. **Botanical Illustration Project**: In this last book, the chapters are named after various fruits and vegetables harvested by farm workers.

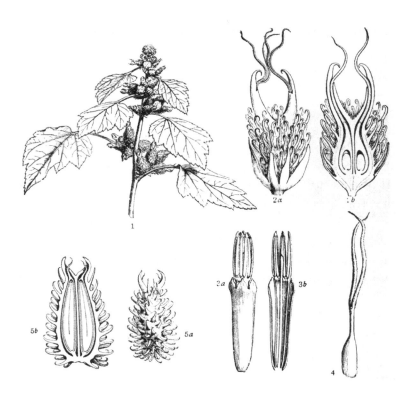

Source: Ladislav František Čelakovský, "Xanthium," in *Ottův Slovník Naučný* (Otto's
Encyclopedia), Vol. 27 (Praha: J. Otto, 1908), 324, accessed May 7, 2018,
https://upload.wikimedia.org/wikipedia/commons/d/d9/Xanthium%2C_parts_of_the_plant.jpg,
public domain.

In this project, students will create books with botanical drawings and
information, much like the illustration above.

Big Question: What can art teach us about science?

Materials list:

- Markers, colored pencils, watercolors, or other color drawing or
  painting media
- Graphite pencil (normal pencil)

- All or some of fruits listed below (alternate idea – use Google Images to draw from photos of fruit)

- Exacto blade or knife

- Microscope

- 4x6 Index cards

- Masking tape

- Optional: 9x12 paper for mounting illustrations

- String or ribbon to bind book

- Hole punch

- Library books on botanical drawing, fruit, and plants – see list below

(a) **Obtain 4 types of books from library:**

  - An advanced or historical adult botanical illustration book, such as:
    Botanical Art: From the Golden Age of Scientific Discovery by Anna Laurent, *Botanical Illustration: The Essential Reference* by Carol Belanger Grafton, or *The Art of Botanical Illustration* by Lys de Bray

  - A beginner botanical illustration book, such as:
    Botanical Illustration for Beginners: A Step-by-Step Guide by Meriel Thurstan & Rosie Martin

  - A book soley on fruit, such as:
    Seeds and Fruits by Melanie Waldron or *The World of Plants: Fruits and Vegetables* by Carrie Branigan and Richard Dunne

  - A general reference book about plants, such as:
    World of Plants: Usborne Internet-linked Library of Science by Laura Howell, et al.

(b) Have students look at an adult botanical illustration book and discuss the following:

  - Which drawings do you like the best, and why?

  - What parts of plants does the artist include?

- Find a picture that has all parts of the plant (seeds, leaves, flower, and fruit) in one picture. Let students know this is the type of drawing they will create for this project.

(c) **Plant Overview:** Using fruit and plant books above, plus *Audubon* (pages 97 and 133-136), spend time researching plants.

Research and Discuss

- What are the two types of true (vascular) plants, and what is the defining characteristic?
  gymnosperms (vascular plants that produced exposed seeds such as confiers) and angiosperms (flowering plants that produce covered seeds)

- How does a flowering plant work? How does it pollinate and what happens when the seeds are mature?

  A flowering plant often contains brightly colored petals that draw pollinators such as insects and birds. Once the pollen from the stamen (male part) gets shaken loose off the anther, it goes to the female part where it sticks on the stigma and is transported down the style to the ovary where it meets the ovules and fertilizes. Once fertilized, these ovules grow and the ovary becomes the fruit. The petals fall off. Eventually the fruit gets heavy and may fall off or be eaten by an animal. The seeds end up on the ground where they are planted and begin their life cycle again.

- What are the major parts of a plant? Fill in Parts of a Flowering Plant, figure B.18, and label the following on the flowering plant diagram: root, stem, leaves, pistil (stigma, style, ovary), stamen (anther, filament), petal, and sepals. Students will return to the seed later.

  Key for figure B.18: 1) stigma 2) style 3) ovary 4) petal 5) anther 6) filament 7) sepal 8) leaves 9) stem 10) roots 11) pistil 12) stamen

- What exactly is a "fruit?" Have students write a paragraph explaining this in their Composition Books. They will add this paragraph to the beginning of their book.

  A fruit is the seed cover (or suitcase) which swells to protect the seed after it has been fertilized. Fruits are unique as they have a symbiotic relationship with animals. Fruit bearing plants are often dependent on animals ingesting the outer seed cover (the fruit) for the seeds to disperse. Think about a deer eating berries and the seeds exiting the deer through droppings left on the ground.

- What are the parts of a seed? Look at Parts of a Seed, figure B.19. Label the following: root (radicle), new shoot (plumule), seed coat (testa), food store.

Answer key:

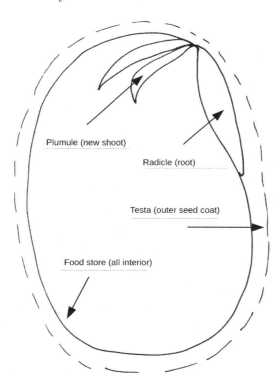

Plumule (new shoot)

Radicle (root)

Testa (outer seed coat)

Food store (all interior)

- What are the two types of fruits? *wet fruit such as melons and dry fruit such as nuts*
- How is a vegetable different from fruit?
  A vegetable is a part of the plant, such as the stem or leaf (asparagus or spinach). Other vegetables, such as cauliflower or broccoli, are the flower of the plant. A tomato is actually a fruit, as it contains fertilized seeds.

(d) **Project:** Obtain each fruit or vegetable that corresponds to each chapter title. An adult should cut open (or bisect) each fruit, slicing through the widest part. Students will draw a crossection of the inside of each fruit or vegetable. Student may alternatively use Google Images to draw from a photo of cut open fruit.

List of fruits in *Esperanza Rising*:

- Grapes
- Papayas
- Figs
- Guavas
- Cantaloupe
- Onions
- Almonds
- Plums
- Potatoes
- Avocados
- Asparagus
- Peaches

(e) With each fruit, students should notice the seeds (and the number of them), their pattern of connection, the skin, and the fleshy, sweet part.

(f) Pull one of the seeds out, and help students cut it open with a knife or an exacto blade. (An adult should use the exacto blade.) Can you see the parts from the seed diagram?

(g) If you have a microscope, offer it to students to explore the seeds, fruit, and rinds.

(h) Look at American Society of Botanical Artists for other good examples of botanical art.

http://www.asba-art.org/

(i) You may choose to do all or only a few fruits. Students should draw a picture of the inside of each fruit and at least one other aspect of the plant, such as the leaves, seed, root, petals, stem, or flower in their Sketch Books, in the style of the sample botanical drawing at the beginning of the chapter. Students may need to use Google Images or a plant book to draw other aspects of the plant.

(j) On a 4x6 card, students should write 5-7 sentences for each fruit or vegetable. Students can go to:

http://www.learnaboutag.org/resources/fact.cfm

to get information about the growing cycle and other facts about most of these fruits.

(k) Students should research the following (list also appears in Student Folder as "Botanical Study Notes," table A.31):

- Name of fruit
- How many seeds?
- What counties (or countries) it grows in
- Lifecycle notes
- Challenges in growing
- Historical facts about the fruit
- Any other interesting facts

(l) Have students tape the card with information on the back of each drawing with removable masking tape.

(m) Using Sketch Books, students should create a cover for their botanical book with a title, name, and date.

(n) Once students finish all of their fruits, have them remove their drawings from their Sketch Books. Either mount drawings on larger paper, such as 9x12 paper, or simply punch 3 holes in the left-hand side of the Sketch Book pages and bind with string or ribbon. Be sure to include the paragraph on how plants and fruits work and their plant and seed diagrams. Informational 4x6 cards can remain taped on the back of the fruit drawings, or mounted on their own sheet of paper and placed near each respective fruit drawing.

3. **Quiet Action Project**: Student will learn how to either crochet or start a rose plant in the garden. Both of these activities, as students will notice in reading this book, are important themes woven into this story. Materials will vary.

Big Question: What can we learn from doing a project?

Growing Roses   Visit The Old Farmer's Almanac. This site features detailed information on cultivating roses, and is easy to read. For more resources, check gardening stores, botanic gardens, and even large retailers such as Home Depot. They often offer classes in planting roses.

https://www.almanac.com/plant/roses

Crocheting   Many craft or fabric stores such as Michael's or JoAnn Fabrics offer classes, which is an ideal way to gain an introduction to this new skill. Also, if there is a local yarn store around where students live, inquire about classes as they often offer them. The following video, *Learn how to crochet for beginners, #1*, by Lisa needlecrafts demonstrates some of the basic stitches.

https://www.youtube.com/watch?v=ZdK-WWdHCQU

Writing Have students write 2-3 paragraphs about how they have learned to do either of these skills. What did they know before they started? What are some of their frustrations they experienced during learning? What did the final creation or plant look like?

4. **Hopes and Dreams Project**: As students read *Esperanza Rising*, they will keep a journal about Esperanza's hopes and dreams in their Composition Books. Students should write the chapter title and date each entry. After reading the book, have students compare Esperanza at the end to the person she was at the beginning of the story. How have her hopes changed?

Some questions to ask while reading:

What does she like? What does she look forward to, hope for, and pray for?

Some hopes and dreams:

- *Las Uvas* - She might become *Las Patronas*, head of household someday; she has a box for *algun dia*, items when she gets married; and she's excited about a *quinceñera* and her 13th birthday.

- *Las Guayabas* - On the train she sees a shrine and misses Papa; nopales cactus reminds her of Abuelita; a dog reminds her of friend Marisol; and she misses her old life in Mexico.

- *Las Cebollas* - She hopes Abuelita will come and bring money to buy them a house.

- *Las Almendras* - She prays for Papa's memory, for Miguel to get a job, for help in taking care of Pepe and Lupe, and she wants white coconut candy.

- *Las Papas* - She wants Abuelita to be there, Mama to get well, work for herself, and soft hands.

- *Las Aguacates* - Esperanza tells Miguel that if he does good work, others will see his efforts and hire him; she is getting money orders to bring Abuelita there.

- *Las Duraznos* - She prays for Marta and Mama; she wishes she could lend Isabel a dress (and wants Isabel to get awarded Queen of May); and she wants a swimming pool.

- *Las Uvas* - She wants to learn English someday, support her family, and get a tiny house.

5. **Simile, Metaphor, & Proverb Gathering Project**: As students read this book, students will keep a journal and write down examples of figurative language such as similes and metaphors, as well as proverbs from the story.

Big Question: Why speak in proverbs?

Discuss: Proverbs, according to Muñoz Ryan, are sayings that are meant to advise or guide. One example is "The grass is always greener on the other side of the fence." What do you think this statement means? *It usually seems like someone else has it better, but the reality is often that we ourselves have things just as good, if not better.*

The author has a section on proverbs at the back of the book under "Those Familiar Sayings." There are also some proverbs in the front pages. Read these with students and unpack their meaning before starting the book.

Metaphor is a form of figurative language similar to simile, but the words "like" and "as" are not used. Some examples include: "The classroom was a zoo" and "He's a night owl."

As students read the story, encourage them to notice the images and objects the author uses. What are the metaphors/similes referring to and what do the proverbs mean? Have students note the chapter, write down the metaphors/similies or proverbs as they read the story, and date each entry.

The following is a list of possibilities:

- *1924* - "Our land is alive," page 1. "Wait a little while and the fruit will fall into your hand," page 2.

- *Las Uvas* - Esperanza is pricked by a thorn which means bad luck; "There is no rose without thorns," page 14.

- *Los Papayas* - Rosehips contain memories of plants and drinking tea made from them enables you to take in all the beauty the plants have known, page 35. "In Mexico we stand on different sides of the river," page 37.

- *Los Higos* - "Do not be afraid to start over," page 49. They are like a phoenix "rising again, with new life ahead of [them]," page 50.

- *Las Guayabas* - The train had bench seating "like church pews facing each other," page 66.

- *Las Cebollas* - The house they live in with Hortensia and Alfonso in California reminds Esperanza more of "horse stalls on the ranch than a place to live," page 100.

- *Las Aguacates* - Esperanza's hands "were the hands of a poor *campesina*," page 182.

- *Las Duraznos* - "Wait a little while and the fruit will fall into your hand," page 223.

- *Las Uvas* - The wounded bird that Abuelita notices gets better and she knows that whatever was wrong with Esperanza and Mama was better, page 245.

6. **Journey Mapping Project**: In this project, students will use Esperanza's Journey Map, figure B.20, and map Esperanza's journey from her town in Mexico to the city where she settles in California. Make notes about her journey. Mark the path and label the cities she stops at on the map. Download and find pictures of these cities on her journey. Students may also draw a few of their favorite scenes. Students can

present a project in a powerpoint presentation or in another medium.

Big Question: Why do we tell others our journeys?

List of cities:

- Aguascalientes, Mexico
- Zacatecas, Mexico (arrives by way of wagon ride)
- Mexicali on US/Mexico order (arrives by way of train)
- Los Angeles, CA (arrives by way of truck)
- Arvin, CA (arrives by way of truck)
- Bakersfield, CA (goes there to visit Mama in the hospital and receive Abuelita)

For map answer key see "Journey Mapping: How We Came," page 218.

Chapter 11

Esperanza Rising

11.1 Week 30

> **Teacher's Note** Comprehension questions are provided, but focus on having students work consistently on the project you/they choose.

Big Question: What is migration?

Read to Students In this last book, like the monarch, you will migrate north from Mexico. Can you remember others who came from Mexico to California? *mission fathers such as Junípero Serra*

As you read this book, pay special attention to Esperanza's experience immigrating to California. What do the places look like on her journey to California? Are they lush or dry areas?

11.1.1 1924 and *Las Uvas*, pages 1-22

Big Question: How do children live in other places? (Murdoch, 2015)

1. What two things does Papa tell Esperanza when she is 6? *If she lays down on the earth, she can feel the earth alive with its heart beating. Also, if she waits a little while, the fruit will fall in her hand.*

2. Where do Esperanza and her family live? Who else lives with them in their house? What is their background? *They live on a rancho in Aguascalientes, Mexico. Her mom–Ramona, dad–Sixto, grandmother–Abuelita, and house servants–Alfonso, Hortensia, and their son Miguel live with her. They also have vaqueros and campesinos at their rancho.*

3. What is a *campesino*? *A campesino is a field worker.*

4. What crop are they harvesting at Rancho de las Rosas in these two chapters? *grapes*

5. What place will Esperanza eventually rise to in her household? *Like her mother, she will rise to las patronas, the head of the household.*

6. They are living in the time period just after the revolution in Mexico. What feelings do people have towards wealthy landowners? *Wealthy landowners are despised.*

Reflection   Esperanza spends time crocheting with her *abuelita*. What are some things about life she learns from Abuelita? *You should never be afraid to start over; there is no rose without thorns; she crochets to take her mind off worries; and even gray hair can be woven into her work.*

11.1.2   *Las Papayas*, pages 23-38

Big Question: How am I connected to my past? (Murdoch, 2015)

1. Who do they find killed Papa? *Bandits killed him as he was mending his fence.*

2. What is Esperanza's favorite salad? How does she make it? *Her favorite salad contains papayas, lime, and coconut.*

3. She eventually opens her gifts from her birthday. What does she find Papa has given her? *Her father has given her a porcelain doll with a white batista and a white lace mantilla.*

4. If Esperanza and Mama stay at Rancho de las Rosas after Papa dies, what will their lives be like? *They get their house, contents, and the income from grapes, but their father's brothers would own their rancho*

land. Her uncles only care about money and increasing their power, as one is a mayor and the other owns the bank that owns the Ortega's land.

5. What did Papa plant for Esperanza and Miguel? What colors? *For Esperanza he plants mini pink roses, and for Miguel, orange sunburst roses.*

6. What can Miguel aspire to if he stays in Mexico? What work will he do? *If Miguel stays in Mexico, all he can aspire to be is a servant. He decides he will go the the US as he will have more opportunities.*

11.1.3 *Los Higos*, pages 39-57

Big Question: What makes a home? (Murdoch, 2015)

1. What happens to Esperanza's home? Who do they think is behind it? *The uncles have set fire to it.*

2. What does Mama decide she and Esperanza will do? What will Alfonso and Hortensia do? What work will they do? *Because their home burns down, Mama decides she and Esperanza will go to the US and be field workers with Alfonso and Hortensia. Esperanza says she can work too, and they laugh.*

3. Now that they do not have their home, where must they get their necessities such as clothes? *They get clothing from the poor box at the convent.*

4. What does Abuelita tell them about starting over? What journey did her own family take? *Abuelita reminds them to not be afraid to start over as she did. Her dad was from Spain, but he was offered a job in Mexico, so her family came with him to Mexico.*

5. Use the library or look online for a recounting of the Myth of the Phoenix. Put the story in your own words. Google search terms: phoenix myth

   The mythical phoenix is a large colorful bird that, when sensing its end is near, builds a funeral fire and then ignites it. After the fire dies down, the phoenix is reborn and flies away.

11.2   Week 31

11.2.1   *Las Guayabas*, pages 58-80

Big Question: Can we learn anything from older people?

1. How do Sr. Rodriguez, Alfonso, and Miguel make Esperanza's journey safer on their wagon ride to Zacatecas? *They build a false bottom in the wagon that Esperanza and her mother hide in.*

2. What memory does Esperanza have of taking a train ride from Zacatecas with Miguel when he was younger? How does that ride compare with the train ride they eventually now take to get to the United States? *When she was 5 she went on the same route from Zacatecas, only in first class where she had nice tablecloths and silver service.*

   Review   Esperanza sees a beggar lady with a picture of Our Lady of Guadalupe. What do you remember about this story? *The story recounts when the Virgin Mary is said to have appeared to Aztec Juan Diego during the 16th century in Mexico City.*

3. What does Esperanza grow weary of while on the train? *She is tired of Miguel, Hortensia, Alfonso, and even her mother's crocheting.*

4. What opportunities does Miguel think await him in the US versus in Mexico? *He wants to work on a railroad, which he thinks he will be able to do in the US.*

5. When they meet the widow Carmen on the train, how does she describe happiness? Though she is poor, what ways does she say she is rich? *Carmen describes happiness as having family, a garden with roses, faith, and a memory of those gone before her.*

6. What are some things about their old "rich" life that have changed? What activities do they do now that they did not previously do? *Now, Mama tells poor people her business and makes yarn dolls for a poor girl, and she allows Esperanza to eat strangers' food.*

7. What do you think this statement that Miguel says means – "Full bellies and Spanish blood go hand in hand"? Also, what does Miguel

say about people's ethnic color and their wealth? *Miguel's says this because he thinks the Spanish always have enough to eat. He also thinks the more pale (white) a person is, the more money and resources he or she has.*

8. Why do you think Esperanza might see that remark as a wives' tale, and Miguel might think that is simply how the poor see things? *Esperanza might see Miguel's statement as a wives' tale because she IS of Spanish blood. She has never known otherwise. Poor people might agree with him as they do not have privilege and must always work hard to eat.*

11.2.2 *Los Melones*, pages 81-99

Big Question: Can one person make a difference? (Murdoch, 2015)

1. Where are some places they stop after they take the train from Zacatecas? Where do they enter the border? *They stop at the border in Mexicali, then they stop in Los Angeles, and Arvin, and they are headed up the 99 highway into the San Joaquin Valley.*

2. Describe the habitat in the border area – what plants and animals do they see? *At the barren border region, they see palms, cacti, squirrels and roadrunners.*

3. What is the story of Alfonso's brother's family? Where have they lived, and where do they live now? What type of work do they do (and what type of people are they)? Describe their home. *They used to live in El Centro at the border. Now they live in Arvin. They harvest crops and they pay $7 per month for a home in Arvin with electricity, a kitchen, and piped in water. They used to have a home with a dirt floor. They are Mexican.*

4. What type of a person is Marta? What is her ethnic background and social status? *Her father was from Mexico, and he died helping the poor in the Mexican Revolution. Marta is a poor field worker.*

5. How does Marta describe the labor camps? How are they divided? What is a strike? *Marta says that each ethnic group has a different camp to live in. A strike is when workers refuse to work.*

11.2.3 Habitat Study: Deserts

Read to Students As Esperanza and her mother travel to the United States on the train, they go through a desert region.

 Big Question: Are there any similarities in how plants and animals adapt in the same habitat?

1. Use Google Images to look at some pictures of the deserts of Mexico. Google search terms: mexico desert photos

2. What do you see? *cactus, sand, wispy bushes, mountains*

   Read "Deserts" in *Audubon* on pages 38-39.

3. What desert is found in California that is also a part of Mexico? *Colorado Desert: In Mexico it's known as the Sonoran Desert.*

4. What are some examples of how plants and animals have adapted to this challenging environment?

   Mesquite trees have roots that grow as much as 4 inches a day to reach water, the kit fox, desert cottontail, and black-tailed jackrabbit have large ears to help radiate heat away from their body, many plants like the ocotillo drop their leaves in summer so not to lose water.

   Bonus What 3 deserts are mentioned, and what are their average rainfall levels? Make a list:

   - *Great Basin, 8-20 inches*
   - *Mojave Desert, 4-15 inches*
   - *Colorado Desert, 1-5 inches*

5. Fill in Habitat Tracker B for deserts.

6. Students may either complete the Habitat Description Sheet or Native Habitat Home Building Project. If students choose the Habitat Description Sheet, they should draw a picture of the land, a plant, and an animal, and label them; they should also write a short paragraph about this habitat.

Habitat	Trees/Shrubs	Flowering Plants	Animals	Location (cities)
Desert	*Big sagebrush, Joshua tree, smoke tree, creosote bush, blue palo verde*	*Most bushes will flower: including Mojave yucca, creosote bush, blue palo verde*	*Desert tortoise, Mojave ground squirrel, desert bighorn, coyote*	*Use map on inside of Audubon front cover: Needles, Barstow, El Centro, Ridgecrest, Alturas*

Sample description: There are 3 main deserts found in California: the Mojave, the Great Basin, and the Colorado Desert. Trees and plants are sparsely planted and have adapted to living with very low levels of water. The Joshua tree, smoke tree, and the creosote bush are some of the major large trees found. Rabbits, tortoise, sheep, and squirrels all have unique adaptations that enable them to live in this environment.

11.2.4 *Las Cebollas*, pages 100-120

Big Question: What is work and why do people do it? (Murdoch, 2015)

1. Esperanza finally reaches the new place she will live. What does she think of it? How does it compare with her old home? What does her new home remind her of? *The new home where she lives with Alfonso and Hortensia reminds her of horsestalls. It is very small. She and Mama live with Alfonso's family in a small, two-bedroom house.*

2. Mama pulls Esperanza aside and tells her she has two choices about how she can live. According to Mama, what are these choices? *They can live together and be happy, or they can live together and be miserable.*

3. Describe what jobs/work everyone is doing now. What new skills does Esperanza learn? *Miguel looks for work on the train. Others go to work on the fields and school. Mama will work on the fields and Esperanza*

will take care of the children, sweep floors, and do laundry. Esperanza learns how to change diapers and sweep floors.

Reflection If you were in Esperanza's place, how would you feel hearing your mother give you two choices about how you can respond? Have you been a situation like this before, where something didn't go quite right, and you decided to make the best of it – or maybe not to make the best of it? Tell or write this story.

Reflection Imagine yourself in Esperanza's place. If you were her, how would you feel about having to learn these basic skills such as sweeping at age thirteen?

11.2.5 Journey Mapping: How We Came

Big Question: What makes a journey a journey?

Have students look at Google Earth and find the city of Arvin. **Google search terms: arvin california map**

On Esperanza's Journey Map, figure B.20, have students draw the line of the journey from Aguascalientes to Zacatecas to Mexicali (Mexican bordertown, where Esperanza enters the United States), to Los Angeles, and finally to Arvin.

Add Esperanza to How We Came Tracker, table A.14.

Esperanza's Journey Map answer key:

11.3 Week 32

11.3.1 *Las Almendras*, pages 121-138

Big Question: Why do people pray?

1. What does Esperanza find Miguel and Alfonso have created in back of their house? What parts of the display do you recognize? Have students draw a picture in Sketch Books of what they imagine the altar looks like. *The have rescued the roses bushes from Aguascalientes and replanted them in the camp, giving them water along the journey. In the altar, there is a Mary statue from Josefina and roses from home.*

2. Esperanza learns more about Marta's ethnicity and where they live. Where does she find Marta is from, and what does it mean that she

is a migrant laborer? *Marta and her mother are citizens of the United States and they have never been to Mexico. Her father though was from Sonora, Mexico. She is a migrant worker, which means she moves from camp to camp finding work and housing.*

3. At the end of the chapter, Esperanza and Mama pray for some of their hopes. What things do they pray/hope for? *Esperanza prays for Papa's memory, that Miguel gets a train job, for help in taking care of the babies, Pepe and Lupe, and for white coconut candy. Mama prays that Esperanza will be strong no matter what.*

11.3.2 *Las Ciruelas*, pages 139-157

Big Question: What is a "good education?" (Murdoch, 2015)

1. In this chapter, the farm workers are caught in a dust storm. What happens in this weather event and how can people stay safe? *In dust storms, sometimes trucks come in time to get the workers safely off the fields. In this case, they did not. When staying in buildings, to seal inside spaces, people put towels under doors and stay away from windows as they might break. When the storm ends, the wind stops first, then the dust.*

2. What happens to Mama as a result of the dust storm? *Mama has valley fever; dust spores have accumulated in her lungs.*

Reflection If you were Esperanza, how might you feel staying home and doing all of the chores, while Isabel goes to school?

11.3.3 Habitat Study: Grasslands of the Central Valley

In *Las Ciruelas*, Esperanza experiences first-hand what life is like in the Central Valley.

Read *Audubon*, "Grasslands of the Central Valley" on pages 40-41.

  Big Question: How are plants and animals the same and different? (Murdoch, 2015)

1. What adaptation have grasses made to survive being grazed by herbivores? *They grow from the base of the plant, not the tip; if grazed by animals they can still grow.*

2. Why do few native grasses remain? *When the area was being grazed by cattle, the ranchers brought in non-native grazing forage.*

3. What are some dominant plants? *poppies, lupines, goldfields, wild oats grass*

4. What animals are found in this habitat? *kit foxes, American kestrals, greater roadrunner, California quail, black-tailed jackrabbit*

5. Use Google Images to look at some pictures of the grasslands. What colors of flowers and trees and landforms do you see? Google search terms: california central valley grassland photos

   Colors and landforms: green, brown, yellow, orange hills, few trees, relatively flat land

6. Fill in Habitat Tracker B (table A.4) for grasslands.

Habitat	Trees/Shrubs	Flowering Plants	Animals	Location (cities)
Grasslands	*Red brome, wild oats, filarees, goldfields*	*California poppies, lupines, coreopsis, owl's clover*	*California quail, black-tailed jackrabbit, tule elk, greater roadrunner*	*Use map on inside of Audubon front cover: Bakersfield, Sacramento, Fresno, Merced*

7. On your Habitat Description Sheet, draw a picture of the land, a plant, and an animal, and label them. Write a short paragraph about this habitat.

Alternatively, students may complete the Native Habitat Home Building Project. Be sure to have students complete the project by mounting photos of 8 habitats in their Sketch Books with habitat titles and an explanation of the materials they used in each structure.

Sample description: The grasslands of the Central Valley feature many grasses that grow because they were planted by cattle ranchers. Many grass species have roots that go far down; they grow from the base of their stem so plants can survive foraging. Some animals found in this habitat include the kit fox, road runner, and tule elk. Poppies, lupines, and various non-native grasses are common.

11.3.4 *Las Papas*, pages 158-178

Big Question: Can we learn anything through being sick?

1. With Mama being sick, Esperanza finds herself in a challenging situation. What gives her strength? *The memory of her abuelita gives her strength. She remembers Abuelita told her to finish the blanket.*

2. Miguel thinks that Esperanza might be able to get work on the farm. What does he advise her to do if she wants to get future work? *He tells her if she is good at one type of work, she will get hired for another.*

3. Once she gets work, how does she keep herself warm? How does she learn to do these things? *Hortensia tells her if she warms a brick and wraps it in a newspaper, she will keep warm. She also wears two pairs of gloves.*

4. What is "cutting potato eyes"? *She cuts two slits in each potato so it has two chances to root.*

Bonus: Cutting Potato Eyes Look up cutting potato eyes online, and find out how this is done. Give it a try! **Google search terms:** cutting potato eyes

5. In her old life at *Rancho de las Rosas*, how did she celebrate Christmas? *In Mexico they set up and advent wreath, and a moss nativity, and they ate empanadas and sweet raisin tamales. After going to mass at midnight, they came back and drank hot chocolate and opened gifts.*

Review Does the way Esperanza celebrates Christmas remind you of any other characters you have studied? *María Rosalia*

6. What does it mean that Esperanza will take on the roll of *la patrona*? *She will be the one who takes care of her mama and works hard to provide for her.*

11.4 Week 33

11.4.1 *Los Aguacates*, pages 179-198

Big Question: Do others see us differently than we see ourselves?

1. In what way does she realize she is like a poor *campesina*? *She has rough hands.*

2. In this chapter, Miguel and Esperanza go to a Japanese market to shop. Why do they choose to shop there? Describe what the inside of the market is like.
   They choose go to the Japanese market because the Japanese are more accepting of Mexicans than Americans are. The Americans see them as a brown group, only good for manual labor. In the market, there are piñatas and Japanese lanterns, as well as other Mexican and Japanese products.

3. From what they see and what Marta says, describe what life is like on the Striker's Farm. *There are guards, and people live in tents with burlap sacks strung between poles. There are even mattresses on the ground.*

4. How might the looming strike change things for the people who choose to work? *Strikers may physically hurt workers who decide to continue working.*

5. What will Miguel do to take advantage of the strike? How does Esperanza encourage him? *Since there will be a strike (and fewer workers), Miguel decides to find work on the railroad. Esperanza tells him if he does good work, others will see this and keep him.*

Reflection   How do different ethnicities both in town and on farms see each other and feel about going to school together? *In town, there is not much mixing as white Americans do not want their kids to go to school with Mexicans. In the camp schools, there is more ethnic mixing because they are all poor.*

11.4.2   *Los Esparragos*, pages 199-213

Big Question: Can conflict be good for relationships? (Murdoch, 2015)

1. The strike has begun, and the people who continue to work are harassed. What does Esperanza want to tell the strikers as she goes to work each day? Why does she keep working? *She works to support her sick mama.*

2. What are some awful things the strikers do to infuriate and scare the workers? *They hide snakes and razor blades in packing crates.*

3. One day, instead of the usual yelling from the strikers, it is dead quiet. What has happened, and where have all the strikers been taken? *The strikers have been rounded up by Immigration and Naturalization Service (INS). They have been bussed to Los Angeles where they will be reunited with their families and taken to Mexico.*

Bonus   What will be their route back to Mexico? *They will go to Los Angeles, ride the train to El Paso, then cross the Mexico border.*

Reflection Esperanza sees Marta hiding amongst the crates. If you were Esperanza, what would you choose to do at that moment? What were her choices, and what do you think of what she decided to do? *She could have told the authorities about Marta, but instead she gave her cover to look like a farm worker.*

Reflection What do you think of the idea that the US sends people back to Mexico who have never lived in Mexico before? If whole families are deported together (some of whom have never lived in Mexico before), how might this impact their lives?

11.4.3 U.S. Citizenship: How to Apply

Teacher's Note This section is more geared towards 5th-6th graders, but younger students can definitely benefit from even a brief website introduction – it's valuable for young students to know that there is a process for immigrants to live in the US, particularly if there has not been recent immigration experience in a student's family.

There are many sources of information available online to answer the questions below. Students may want to type in the exact question and look at several results. Answers will vary.

Big Question: What makes us who we are? (Murdoch, 2015)

Read to Students One of the themes in *Los Esparragos* is that while some people are citizens, others are not. Those who are not live in constant fear of deportation back to Mexico. This is especially difficult for family members who have never lived in Mexico before. Imagine being a child born here with no memory of life in Mexico, and yet fearing being taken there at any time. To get an idea of what immigrants are up against, spend some time exploring the steps to become a citizen. The United States Citizenship and Immigration Services site has a concise PDF that explains the process. Either view online or print out.

`https://www.uscis.gov/sites/default/files/USCIS/files/M-1051.pdf`

Research the following:

1. From the PDF, how many steps are there to become a citizen? *10*

2. From online research, what are the three main paths for non-citizens to obtain work in the US? Google search terms: working in the us

   `https://www.uscis.gov/`
   `working-united-states/working-us`

   Non-citizens must have either a green card, a work permit, or a visa to work with a specific employer.

3. How many people apply for green cards each year? *Answers will vary.*

4. What are the top 5 countries of origination for legal permanent residence (LPR)? *Answers may vary. For 2013 it was Mexico, China, India, the Philippines, and the Dominican Republic.*

5. Applicants for citizenship must take a civics test. If students have covered early through modern US history, have them take the test. The 20 questions should take 20-30 minutes.

   `https://my.uscis.gov/prep/test/civics`

11.4.4 *Los Duraznos*, pages 214-233

Big Question: What is hope?

1. What is Esperanza praying/hoping for? *She prays for her mom and Marta.*

2. Isabel hopes that she will make Queen of May. How does that competition usually work? Who usually wins? What does Esperanza tell her is true, even if she doesn't win? *The girl with the best grades gets the prize, although when it's a girl who is not white, for some reason the blonde girl gets it. Esperanza tells her that even if she does not get it, she is still beautiful.*

3. There is a new camp being built for people coming from Oklahoma. How is it different from the Mexican camp? Under what circumstance are Mexicans allowed in the Okie camp? *The Okie camp has toilets, hot water, and a swimming pool. Mexicans can use the pool on Friday night, just before it gets cleaned Saturday morning.*

4. How are things different on the railroad for Miguel now that more Okies are there? *Okies work for half as much as Mexicans, so they take jobs away from Mexicans.*

5. How long have Esperanza and Mama been in California? *1 year*

6. Does Isabel end up winning the Queen of May competition? What does Esperanza do to cheer her up? *Isabel does not get chosen, so Esperanza gives her the doll she got from Papa.*

Reflection As Esperanza and Miguel are talking, she questions if life is really better for them in the US than in Mexico. Do you think life is better for Esperanza now that she is in the US? For Miguel? For Mama?

11.5 Week 34

11.5.1 *Las Uvas*, pages 234-253

Big Question: What does being successful mean? (Murdoch, 2015)

1. What fruits are families enjoying in this chapter? Which are your favorite? *peaches, plums, nectarines, cantaloupes, coconuts, limes*

2. What surprise does Esperanza get at the bus station? How has she come to Bakersfield? *Her abueltia arrives on a bus. Miguel went to Mexico to bring her to the US.*

3. What time markers does she use to describe the last year to Abuelita? What fruits have come and been harvested by them? *She describes the year by the fruits and vegetables they harvested: grapes, potatoes, asparagus, peaches, plums, etc.*

4. How does she describe happiness now? What things bring her joy? Who else in this story had those things? *She describes happiness as family, a garden full of roses, faith, and the memories of those who went before her. Carmen, the poor beggar woman on the train, introduced her to this idea.*

5. What does she hope for in the future? *She hopes to learn English, support her family, and buy a tiny house.*

6. What does she say to Isabel when Isabel gets frustrated with her crochet? Where does she get this idea from? *Esperanza tells Isabel not to be afraid to start over. She heard this initially from Abuelita.*

Reflection Would those 4 items – family, a garden full of roses, faith, and the memory of those who went before you – bring you happiness? How do you define happiness?

11.5.2 Author's Note

Big Question: What do authors do? What choices do authors make?

1. Who was the author's inspiration for this book? How closely did the story parallel the story of her own grandmother, mother, and father? *The author's grandmother was the inspiration for this book. There are very close parallels between the story of Esperanza and Mama, and the author's own family history.*

2. Why did workers strike in the 1930s? *Workers went on strike because the working conditions were not good; they were not getting paid well.*

3. Is valley fever a real disease? How is the author personally involved with it? *It is a real disease brought on by dust storms. The author found through bloodwork that she tested positive for it, though she had immunity by living in the area.*

4. What is the author's view of how other ethnicities saw the Okies? What were all workers living for? *The author found that there were no intense grudges against Okies. Farm workers were all so poor that they spent most of their time working hard.*

5. What does the word *esperanza* mean? *Esperanza means hope in Spanish.*

Bonus What did the Deportation Act of 1929 cause in the Mexican community? What areas of California were impacted? About how many people were displaced from 1929-1935?

The result of the Deportation Act of 1929 was that anyone who looked Mexican was put on a train and taken to Mexico. Most sweeps took place in Los Angeles and the San Fernando Valley. Sometimes legal naturalized US citizens were caught and sent to Mexico. At least 450,000 people were rounded up and taken to Mexico, though the number could be as high as 1 million.

Add to Timeline

- Year of the Deportation Act *1929*

- Decade of the Dust Bowl (students may need to research this!) *1930s*

11.5.3   Research: Oral History

> **Teacher's Note**   This section gives the basis for the next section, which culminates with each student's family immigration story. Read this section over in it's entirety first, before deciding how you will approach the topic with your students.
>
> For 3rd-4th graders, simplify the steps by having students write up 5-10 interview questions, arrange interview with a family member, record the interview, and write up the information about the immigrated family member. They can skip the more technical aspects and transcription.

Big Question: What does it really mean to listen? (Murdoch, 2015)

Read or Relate to Students   Oral history is a powerful way to capture history. As a worldwide growing body of primary source material, this type of history has been used to gather many unique stories. In oral history, an interviewer designs questions to ask a person of historical interest; these interviews can bring to new light information about the time period or subject matter. Oral histories are often done after times of war or other difficulty as a way to gather stories about peoples experiences who had first-hand knowledge that would otherwise go unrecorded. Most of the time, the stories interviewees tell have not been published. World War II, Vietnam, and Civil Rights era historians have made powerful use of oral history in recording attitudes of the time.

The formal process:

1. The interviewer designs a list of questions for the interviewee. These questions should come from the informational goal of the story and should directly relate to the topic of the interview. For example, if interviewing a person about what life was like in migrant labor camps in the 1930s, it would digress from the goal to ask the interviewee for hours about favorite food or favorite movie. It's important to use the interviewee's time wisely and stay on topic – in this case, his or

her perspective on life in the camps. The interviewer should come up with more questions than needed, as it is easier to omit them in the conversation if the interviewee has already answered the question.

2. Start with general questions and work towards more focused and difficult questions deeper into the interview. The interviewer's goal should be to listen to the answers, not to change the interviewee's mind.

3. The interviewer records the conversation on tape, voice recorder phone app, or other device. The recording device should be reliable; students should verify to make sure it records before the interview. If it is battery operated, the interviewer should bring extra batteries.

4. The interviewer can take notes, but doesn't have to – due to the recorded nature of the interview.

5. The interview is usually transcribed or written out. Transcription occurs in a conversation format, where the interviewer and the subject's words are put into print, similar to the way a courtroom trial is recorded, word for word. This process is useful because the story can be available to historians who are writing books about the time period. Because of transcription, the historian will not have to sift through hours and hours of video or audio recordings. Historians can easily pull out quotes from a transcription.

6. This site gives helpful information on oral history for students in elementary school:

```
http://www.readingrockets.org/article/oral-history
```

11.5.4 Immigration Stories: Migration Is Beautiful

Teacher's Note In this section, using the oral history technique, students will interview a family member.

Big Question: What's my story? (Murdoch, 2015)

Read to Students   You have learned about both the monarch butterfly's journey and Esperanza's journey – both moved between the United States and Mexico.

Discuss with Students   How did you come to live in California? What family member of yours first came here, and when? Why did that person come? What area did he or she settle in? Have you moved from that initial area?

1. In Composition Books, students should make a list of family members who have immigrated to California.

2. After picking one family member to interview, students should design 5-10 questions to ask this family member (more questions for older students). If the immigrated family member is not alive or is unavailable, students can interview parents or other knowledgeable family members to get relevant details.

3. Students will set up and record interviews. For students in 5th or 6th grade, consider having them transcribe interviews.

Complete the How We Came Tracker   Using this oral history information, students will add one last entry in the last row of their How We Came Tracker – their interviewed family member!

11.5.5 Curriculum Culmination: California Butterfly Mobile Project

---

Teacher's Note In this section, students will remember the immigration stories of California and create a mobile as a visual reminder. You may choose to have students add other aspects, such as incorporating habitats and other meaningful symbols. Give additional mobile items some thought before beginning the project.

Big Question: How do people tell their stories? (Murdoch, 2015)

Just as the monarch migrates, so many other characters have migrated to California. Using a monarch butterfly as a symbol of human migration, students will culminate their learning of California migration stories in a mobile project.

Materials list:

- Index cards: 8x5 and 3x5 or 4x6 cards

- Sharpie marker

- Markers, crayons, or colored pencils

- Ribbon or string

- 24" stick from yard/home/hike

- Tape or glue

- Glue gun

1. With a pencil, draw a monarch butterfly on an 8x5 index card. Students may opt to use Butterfly Template in Student Folder (figure B.21). Cover pencil lines with a thick, black Sharpie marker. Make 2 more copies of this butterfly drawing (or template) and mount them on large index cards. Cut out and color 3 butterflies.

2. Have each student find a long stick at or around home, approximately 24 inches long.

3. On three 3x5 cards or 4x6 cards, students will write three shortened versions (3-5 sentences each) about migration stories from the How We Came Tracker, explaining where the person originated from and what route he or she took to get to California, and finally where the person settled:

   - On each card, make the title that person's or character's name
   - One card will have the story of a family member's journey who was interviewed
   - Two other cards should include favorite journeys of characters from the five books (using How We Came Tracker)

4. Students may either glue or tape the small story index cards to the back of the colored butterflies or hang them below butterflies. Put hole punches in the butterflies (and story index cards), and use string to hang them with good spacing on the 24" stick.

5. Add any other items on smaller index cards to the mobile to aid in review. Idea: Have students add 1-3 drawings of their favorite habitats or plants or animals. They will cut these out and hang them on mobile. Students can add any aspects that were meaningful to them.

6. Make an eight-inch wide label that says "California" and cut it out. Students can also draw the letters of "California" and glue-gun letters individually to the stick in order.

7. Using string, have students cut one piece 20 inches long. Tie string to both ends of stick to hang stick mobile.

11.6 Weeks 35-36

11.6.1 Finish Unit V Projects

Teacher's Note Use the last 2 weeks to allow students to finish projects.

11.6.2 Storytelling: *Esperanza* – Hope

Big Question: If we could wave a magic wand, what would we change about the world?

Read one of these stories in *The California Coast* reader (*Stories from Where We Live*):

- "The Long Bike Ride" (page 12)

- "In Trees" (page 119)

Reflect and Discuss the following questions:

1. How have people cared for or wanted to care for nature? How have the kids advocated for or wanted to advocate for nature? What situations have these kids run into? What were they doing initially that took them to the various places?

"The Long Bike Ride": As Antoine is riding his new mountain bike with his friends by the coast near Fort Ord (Monterey area), he discovers a sea lion pup stuck between two rocks. He wants to help rescue it, but he fears the wild animal might bite him. He creates a plan to go back the next day and rescue it, until he hears from his father who is reading a newspaper article that the sea lion was able to swim away on its own, probably because it lost weight.

"In Trees": While Laurel is on her way to her father's house on a Saturday morning, a neighbor tells her that men from the county condemned some redwood trees near the coast on her property. Laurel's father is an arborist who's been having a difficult time since his divorce. She convinces her despondent father to take a look at the trees and thin them so the trees do not need to be cut down.

2. Have students review Habitat Tracker A and Habitat Tracker B. What habitat is described in the story you read? What landforms, trees, and plants give you those clues?

"The Long Bike Ride": This story takes place both in the coast and coastal scrub habitats. The author mentions cypress trees, sand dunes, seastars, rocky shores, and thorny shrubs.

"In Trees": This story takes place in the (coastal) coniferous forest. Laurel talks about the redwood trees she's trying to save, which grow 5-35 miles from the coast, mostly in northern California. It's wet and foggy there.

Hope Storytelling

Writing Project   Have a discussion with students about a situation where they have encountered wild nature that impacted them, and like these stories, they wanted to do something. They can also consider any local or urban issues that have concerned them.

Students should write 1-3 paragraphs describing this story, and write about an action they could take, even if they did not take action at the time.

Students should give details about what place (habitat) their story is located in. Who were they with?

11.6.3 Timeline Completion

Teacher's Note Students have finished adding events to the timeline. If students have created their timeline on cards, have students arrange the cards in chronological order. Create one card with a title for the California timeline and the student's name. Using 6" wide banner paper, lay cards out either horizontally or vertically and tape them to the banner paper in order. For the Timeline Key, see table C.4.

If students have used Timetoast, have them print out their work.

Review Using their timeline, have students either tell you or write out the California story.

11.6.4 End of Unit V and End of Curriculum Questions

Questions for further consideration:

1. What will you not forget from studying California?

2. In what ways does Esperanza embody what her name means in Spanish, "hope"? Remember her beginnings as a wealthy girl of privilege, and emerging by the end of the story as a poor *campesina*. What are some of the major losses early on, and what have those been replaced with by the end of the story? How has she found reasons to hope?

   Initially, she lives on a wealthy rancho with her mother and father and servants. Papa gets killed; she and Mama must flee their rancho in Mexico using clothes from the poor box at church to break free from her two corrupt uncles. By the end of the story, she believes family, faith, a garden of roses, and the memories of those who have gone before her will bring her happiness.

   Esperanza also believes wisdom that others have shared with her along the way: Papa told her that if she is patient, fruit will fall into her hand. Abuelita tells her to never be afraid to start over. Miguel lets her know that if she works hard, she will get hired to do more work.

3. Miguel says, "Full bellies and Spanish blood go hand in hand." Do you believe this statement is true? As you reflect back on *Island of the Blue Dolphins* and *Valley of the Moon*, has this been shown to be true in the characters of Esperanza, María Rosalia, and Karana? Do people with paler skin do better? If so, why do you think this is?

   Yes, people with pale skin do better. For example, Karana ends up dying after contact with people at the mission, while the Russians and mission fathers do not. In María Rosalia's case, early on she is a servant. When she finds she has Spanish background, her fortune improves and she acquires property. In Esperanza's case, in Mexico as a girl of Spanish background, she had much wealth. When she comes to the US

as a Mexican national, she loses her Spanish privilege as she is seen as
Mexican. Answers will vary about why pale people do better.

4. There are many projects about immigration reform that have used the symbol of the monarch butterfly. Journey North created a symbolic migration project through which students at schools in the US create ambassador butterflies. In the fall each year, after taking photo of themselves with their butterflies, students ship their ambassador butterflies to Mexico. Students can track their butterflies through the Journey North website. In Mexico, students hold and protect the butterflies and ship them back to the US carrying special messages for US students. Visit this site to read some of the stories:

   `https://www.learner.org/jnorth/symbolic-migration`

5. Imagine you are born in another country at some point in a time period you have studied. You decide you would like to come to California. How do you come? What risks do you face during this historical period? What draws you to California? Write a letter to a family member about your journey to California. What do you miss most about home?

6. Which of the major characters from our 5 books have you most identified with, and why – Karana, María Rosalia, Jack, Chin, Henry, Miguel, or Esperanza? What do you admire about that character? What do you like about the time period he or she lived in?

7. Pick one character from your How We Came Tracker, and write a paragraph in your Composition Book describing how climate, amount of water (or lack of water), and habitat has influenced his or her life. How have the native plant and animal life around this character influenced the type of shelter, food, and clothing he or she wears?

8. **Formal Review Essay Option for 5th/6th Graders**: For an oak tree to grow, it needs enough water, ample sunlight, and organic nutrients. Without these resources it would never grow. Just as the oak tree sends up sprouts, so California has flourished. From your study of this state, what conditions have fostered an ever-increasing population boom in the Golden State? Why have so many come here?

Write a formal essay. Pick 2-3 details that support your hypothesis as to why people have risked their lives to settle here. Use Student Folder to review all maps, habitats, stories, climate and precipitation, population growth, geology, and data projects.

Write 2-3 paragraphs; in each paragraph state one of the reasons for growth. Arrange paragraphs in a logical order. Include an introduction and a conclusion. Choose a quote from one of the books that gives a flavor of your opinion.

Sample reasons why California has grown: A) geographic location: California sits on the border with Mexico and is located on the Pacific Ocean where people have arrived by boat from other countries. B) Mineral resources: Due to the rock cycle and mineral wealth such as gold, people have come with dreams of owning a portion. C) Timeline: Compared to the rest of the US and Mexico and South and Central America, California developed much later, not even attaining statehood until 1850. Because of late development, there was room for more people than other more developed states/countries.

Appendices

Appendix A

Tables for Student Folder

Animal	Place	Date	Season	The animal was ...

Table A.1: Animals and Habitats

People Group	Foods	Type of work they are doing	Nature they interact with	Weapons	Other Notes

Table A.2: Groups on San Nicolas Island

Habitat	Trees/Shrubs	Flowering Plants	Animals	Location (cities)
Coast & Islands				
Chaparral & Coastal Scrub				
Oak Woodlands				
Sierra Nevada				

Table A.3: Habitat Tracker A

Habitat	Trees/Shrubs	Flowering Plants	Animals	Location (cities)
Coniferous Forest				
Marsh				
Desert				
Grasslands				

Table A.4: Habitat Tracker B

Habitat: ————————————————————————————

Table A.5: Habitat Description

Directions: Draw the land, a plant, and an animal; label each one. Write a paragraph about each habitat.

Sample Number	Tree Shape	Leaf Shape	Leaf Arrangement	Flower Type	Flower Cluster Type	Identi- fication
1						
2						
3						
4						
5						
6						
7						
8						
9						
10						

Table A.6: Plant Observations

English	Chosen Language:_____

Table A.7: Language & Word Comparison

1. Year that 18 Native Americans were brought from the island to mainland CA: _____

2. The people who wanted the Native Americans taken to the mainland were the _____

3. Number of years that it is estimated that the "lone woman" lived on the island alone: _____

4. They think she may have dived off the boat to rescue her _____

5. The types of clothing she wore: _____

6. Nature that she could silence: _____

7. The name of the tribe she was a part of: _____

8. Name of the Captain who rescued her: _____

9. Year she was rescued: _____

10. Number of weeks she lived after being rescued: _____

11. Reasons they think she died: _____

12. When she was rescued, how was she able to communicate? _____

13. Mission where she is buried: _____

14. The name they gave to her: _____

Table A.8: Lone Woman History

Source	Primary or Secondary?	Fiction or Nonfiction?
Newspaper article about California becoming a state, written in 1850		
Island of the Blue Dolphins		
Native American's oral history about his or her tribal traditions		
A book about California history written in 2015		
Captain Nidever's journal		

Table A.9: Types of Sources

Pleistocene Animal	Modern Animal Equivalent	How are the two different?

Table A.10: Animals: Pleistocene vs. Modern

1. Title Page:

   - Complete title
   - Authors' names
   - Publisher and city
   - Year published

2. Table of Contents:

   - How many parts?
   - Names of parts
   - Your favorite section (sections are in bold):
   - If you wanted to find out more about mushrooms, what page would you turn to?

3. Index

   - What page does this start on?
   - How is it organized?
   - If I wanted to find out more about Lake Tahoe, what pages could I turn to?
   - Find an animal, bird, or state or national park you like. What pages could you turn to to find out more about it?

4. Acknowledgements

   - What page does this section start on? Hint: use the Table of Contents
   - What type of information do you learn about the authors in this section?
   - Name a group or institution that helped the authors with their research.
   - Why should a reader review this section?

Table A.11: Using the *Audubon* Guide

1. Name and location of the mission

2. What is its informal name, if any?

3. When was it built? Who founded it?

4. Who is the patron saint?

5. Draw the floor plan

6. Who built it?

7. What tribe(s) lived there?

8. How many converts (*neophytes*) were there?

9. Does it have any notable industries?

10. Other interesting facts

11. Include a photo of the mission

Reflection Imagine how a child who is Native American might live differently after spending time at a mission? After only knowing the mission, would he or she be able to go back and live with their tribe?

Table A.12: Mission Research

Character	*californio*	*americano*
Señor Medina		
Captain Frémont		
Señor Villareal		
Henry Johnston		
Johann Sutter		
Gregorio		
Lupita		
Rosalia		
Walter Johnston		
Mariano Vallejo		
Domingo		
Nelly Johnston		
Padre Ygnacio		
Miguela		

Table A.13: *Californio* Table

Character	Birthplace	Migrates to	Method of transportation	Time it took to migrate	Other notes
Karana					
Rosalia					
Junípero Serra & Sacred Expedition					
Walter & Nelly Johnston					
Jack & Praisewor-thy					
Cut-Eye Higgins					
Chin & Ah Sing					
Esperanza					

Table A.14: How We Came Tracker

Item	Karana	Rosalia
Homes		
Tools		
Foods		
Other		

Table A.15: Unit I & II Review

Year	Number of Native Americans in California (estimated and rounded to thousands)
1770	310,000
1830	245,000
1845	150,000
1855	50,000
1880	20,000
1900	15,000
1910	20,000
1933	22,000
1955	36,000
1960	39,000
1970	91,000

Source: Sherburne F. Cook, "Historical Demography," in *Handbook of North American Indians, Vol. 8: California* ed. Robert F. Heizer (Washington, D.C.: Smithsonian Institution, 1978), 91-98.

Table A.16: Population of Native Americans in California, 1770-1970

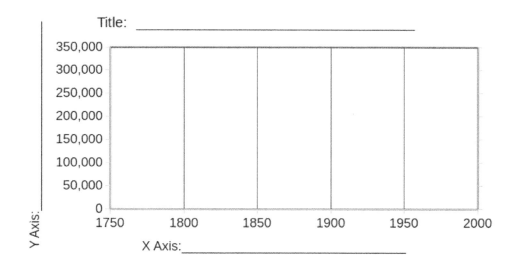

Table A.17: Native Americans in California Chart

Attempt #	Start date	End date	How	Notes	Clipping Result

Table A.18: Water Potato Observations

	Before Journey (Boston)	On the Gold Fields
Praiseworthy		
Jack		
Home		
Foods		
How they spend their time		
Other		

Table A.19: Jack's and Praiseworthy's Change

Oh Susanna!
(Gold Rush Version)

I come from Salem City, with my washbowl on my knee,
I'm going to California, the gold-dust for to see.
It rained all day the day I left, the weather it was dry,
The sun so hot I froze to death – oh, brothers, don't you cry!

Chorus:
Oh, California
That's the land for me!
I'm going to San Francisco
With my washbowl on my knee.

I jumped aboard the 'Liza ship and traveled on the sea,
And every time I thought of home I wished it wasn't me!
The vessel reared like any horse, that had of oats a wealth;
I found it wouldn't throw me, so I thought I'd throw myself!

Chorus

I thought of all the pleasant times we've had together here
I thought I ort to cry a bit, but couldn't find a tear.
The pilot bread was in my mouth, the gold-dust in my eye,
And though I'm going far away, dear brothers, don't you cry!

Chorus

I soon shall be in Frisco, and there I'll look round,
And when I see the Gold lumps there I'll pick them off the ground.
I'll scrape the mountains clean, my boys.
I'll drain the rivers dry,
A pocketful of rocks bring home – so brothers, don't you cry!

Chorus

Table A.20: *Oh Susanna!* Lyrics

Source: Chas. F. Lummis, "Oh Susanna," in *Out West: A Magazine of the Old Pacific and the New*, Vol. XXI (July to December 1904): 271, public domain.

Project: Pick one state or national park. Using *Audubon,* the Internet, and/or library references, write three paragraphs about park of choice. Cover the following details:

1. Date it became a state or national park

2. Location: what cities and freeways is it close to?

3. Activities: walking, skiing, swimming, camping, etc

4. Habitat: information about the wildlife, plants, trees

5. History: what memorable events occurred in this park?

6. Climate: rain, temperature, etc.

7. Why did you choose it? What do you like most about it?

8. Photos: include some photos of the park

Table A.21: Parks Research

Year	Population	Growth Rate
1850		
1860		
1870		
1880		
1890		
1900		

Table A.22: California Population Growth (1850-1900)

City	Precipitation	Rank	Population	Rank
	Year:		Year:	
Sacramento				
San Francisco				
Santa Barbara				
Monterey				
Los Angeles				
San Diego				
#1				
#2				
#3				

Table A.23: Average Annual Precipitation & Population

	Plate
1	
2	
3	
4	
5	
6	
7	
8	
9	

Table A.24: Earth's Major Tectonic Plates

Mineral	Hardness
Talc	1
Gypsum	2
Calcite	3
Flourite	4
Apatite	5
Orthoclase	6
Quartz	7
Topaz	8
Corundum	9
Diamond	10

Table A.25: Mohs Hardness Scale

Source: Steven Schimmrich, "Mohs Scale of Hardness," *Hudson Valley Geologist*, August 31, 2010, accessed July 12, 2018, http://hudsonvalleygeologist.blogspot.com/2010/08/mohs-scale-of-hardness.html.

Sample #	Estimated Hardness	Rock Type: Igneous, Sedimentary, or Metamorphic	Notes
1			
2			
3			
4			
5			
6			
7			
8			

Table A.26: Rock Hardness Observation Chart

Sample #	Fracture, Cleavage, or Both	Rock Type: Igneous, Sedimentary, or Metamorphic	Notes
1			
2			
3			
4			
5			
6			
7			
8			

Table A.27: Rock Fracture/Cleavage Observations

	Date	Magnitude	Location	Number of Deaths
1				
2				
3				
4				
5				
6				
7				
8				

Table A.28: California's Largest Earthquakes

- Note where the dam or water storage area is located.

- Where does the water originate, and where does it go?

- What areas or cities are serviced by the water?

- Which one of the major cities that you initially labeled on your California Map does the water flow to (i.e.; San Francisco, Los Angeles, Sacramento, Monterey, Santa Barbara, San Diego)

- Do you imagine the cities that benefit from this water project would grow as big as they have without this project?

- Any other interesting facts.

Table A.29: Water Project Research Notes

Water Project #1: _____
Notes:

Water Project #2: _____
Notes:

Topic:_____

Audubon Guide	Internet	Library Book
Pages:	Website:	Book Title/Author:
	Date:	Pages:
Notes:	Notes:	Notes:

Table A.30: Research Mash-Up

- Name of fruit

- How many seeds?

- What counties (or countries) it grows in

- Lifecycle notes

- Challenges in growing

- Historical facts about the fruit

- Any other interesting facts

Table A.31: Botanical Study Notes

Appendix B

Figures for Student Folder

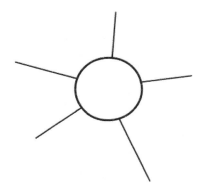

Figure B.1: About Me: Mind Map

Figure B.2: California Map

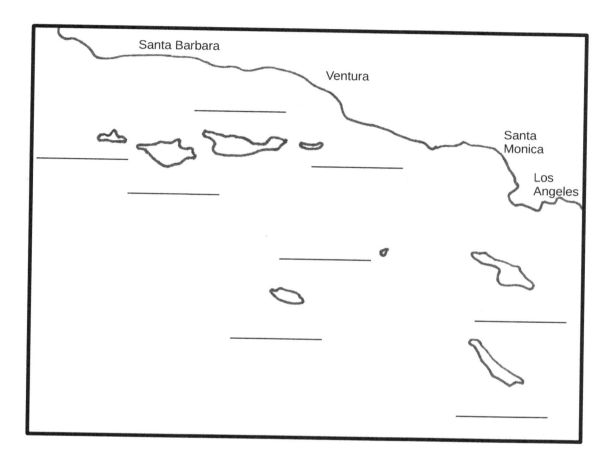

Figure B.3: Channel Islands Map

Fill in the names of each of the islands:

Santa Cruz, Santa Rosa, Anacapa, Santa Catalina, San Miguel,

Santa Barbara, San Nicolas, and San Clemente

Figure B.4: Spain's Land Holdings in the Americas, 18th Century

Source: Jluisrs, "Spanish America XVIII Century," *Wikimedia Commons,* accessed January 29, 2018, https://commons.wikimedia.org/wiki/File:Spanish_America_XVIII_Century_(Most_Expansion).png, public domain.

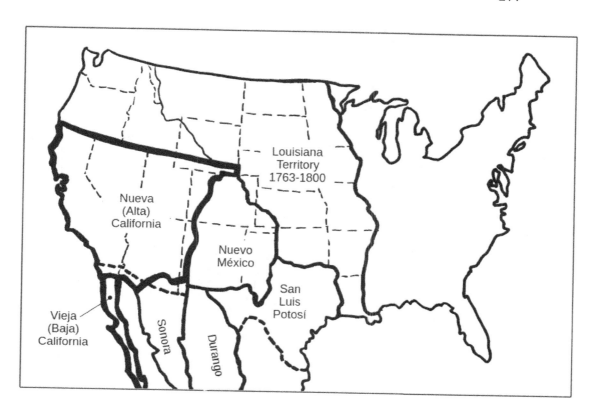

Figure B.5: Northern New Spain Map

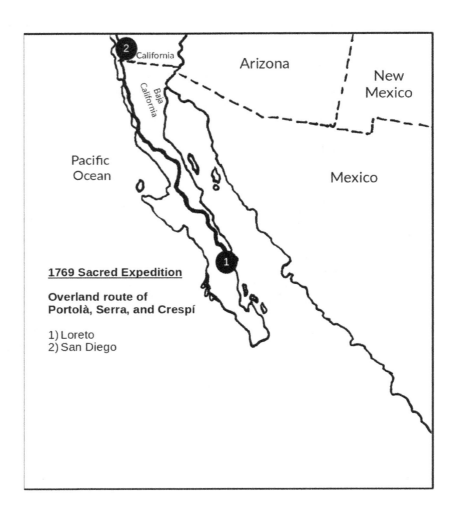

Figure B.6: Map of the Sacred Expedition

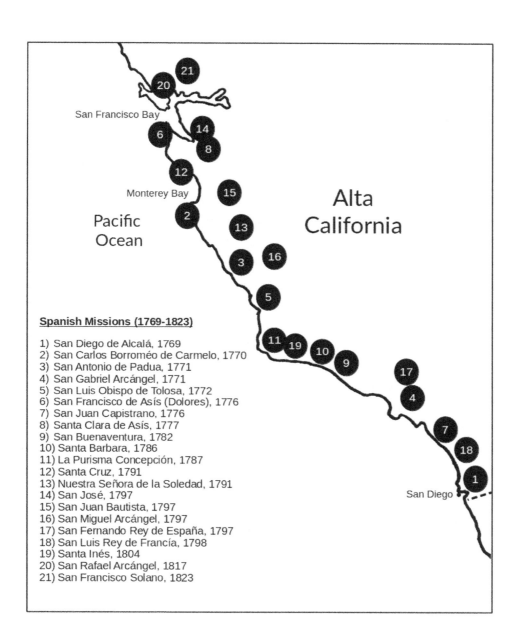

Figure B.7: Map of the Missions

Figure B.8: Map of San Francisco Area

Locate the following and number on the map:

1. Sonoma Mission (Solano)

2. San Rafael Mission

3. San Francisco Mission (de Asís)

4. San Francisco Presidio

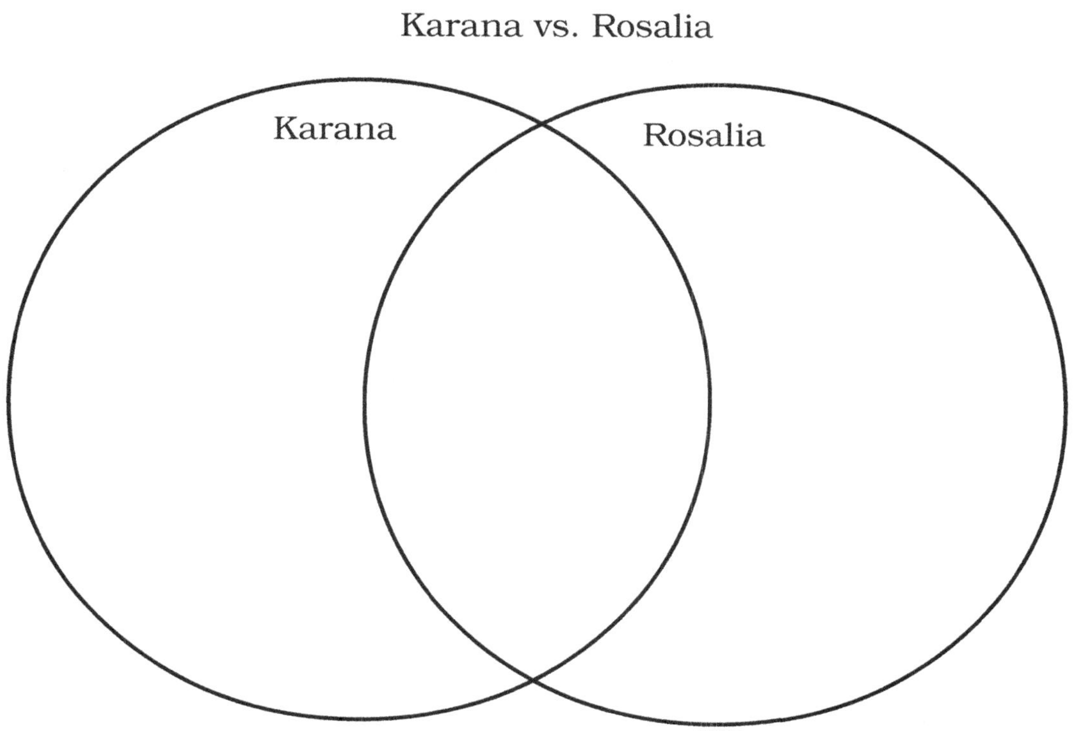

Karana vs. Rosalia

Figure B.9: Venn Diagram: Karana vs. Rosalia

Figure B.10: Map of the Americas

Source: Ceskito, "Blank Americas.png," *Wikimedia Commons*, accessed July 11, 2018, https://commons.wikimedia.org/wiki/File:BlankAmericas.png, public domain.

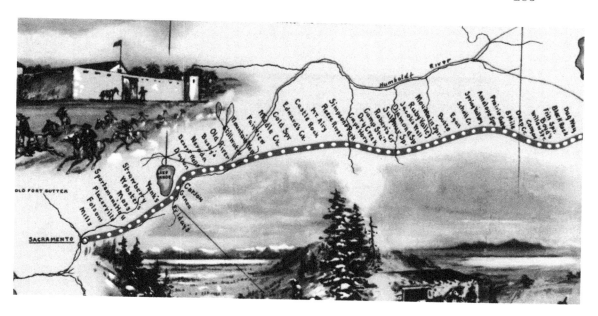

Figure B.11: Map of the Pony Express (Part 1 of 3)

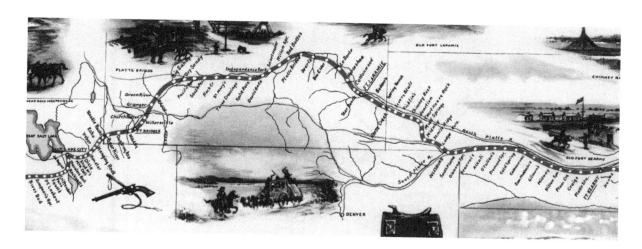

Figure B.12: Map of the Pony Express (Part 2 of 3)

Source for Parts 1, 2 and 3: William Henry Jackson, "Pony Express Map William Henry Jackson.jpg," *Wikimedia Commons*, accessed June 23, 2018, https://commons.wikimedia.org/w/index.php?curid=10111804, public domain.

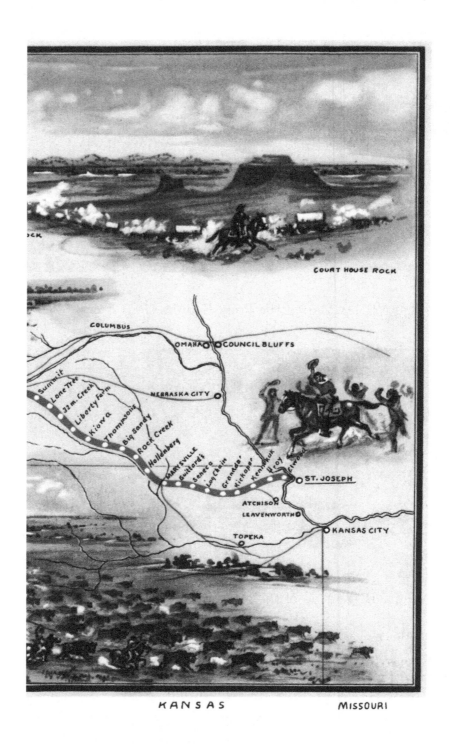

Figure B.13: Map of the Pony Express (Part 3 of 3)

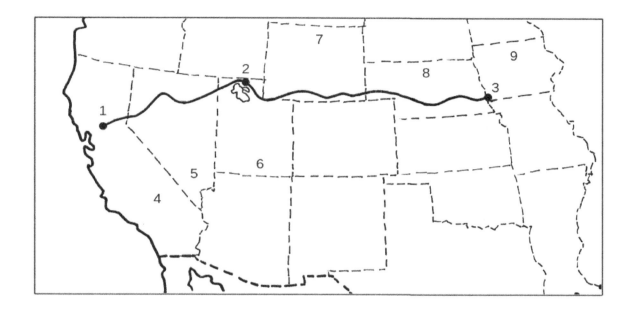

Figure B.14: Transcontinental Railroad Map

Label below: Promontory Summit (Utah), Sacramento (California) and Omaha (Nebraska)/Council Bluffs (Iowa). Also, label the states the railroad passes through. Color and label the Central Pacific line (from #1-2) one color and color and label the Union Pacific Railroad (#2-3) in another color.

1.

2.

3.

4.

5.

6.

7.

8.

9.

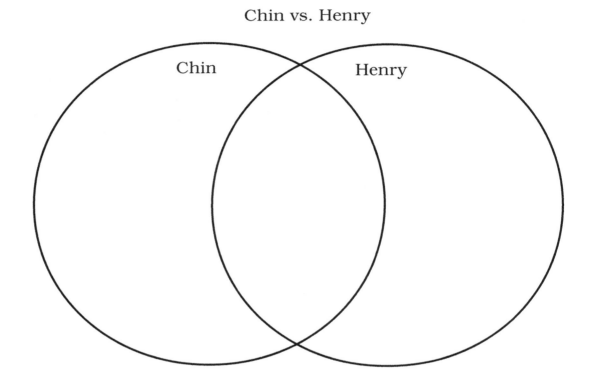

Figure B.15: Venn Diagram: Chin vs. Henry

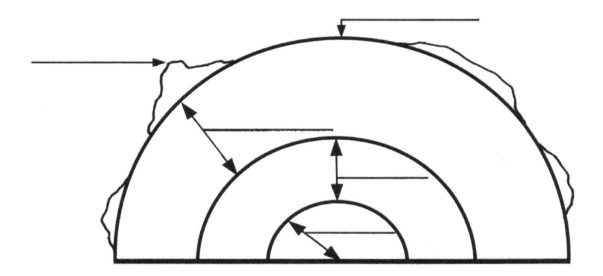

Figure B.16: Layers of the Earth Diagram

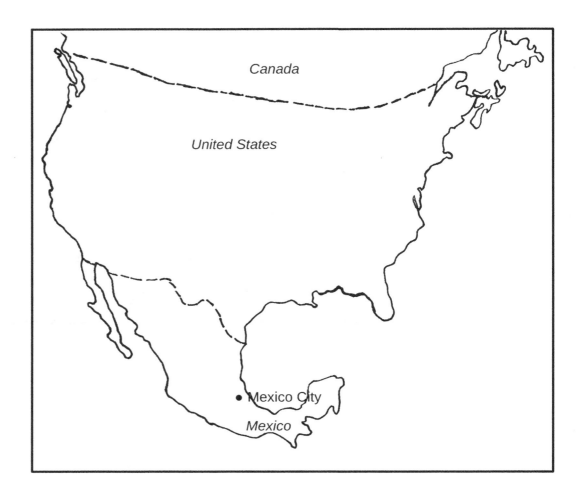

Figure B.17: Monarch Migration Map

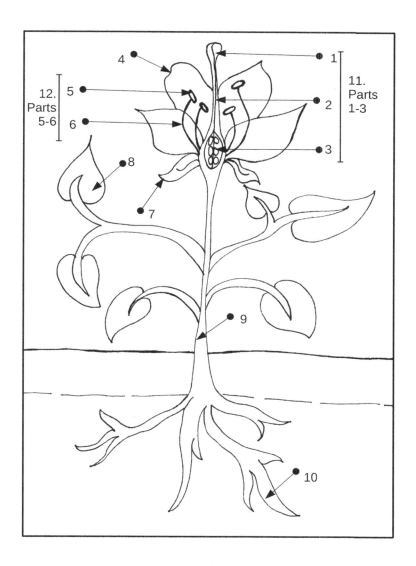

Figure B.18: Parts of a Flowering Plant

Locate and number: root___, stem___, leaves___, pistil___ (stigma___, style___, ovary___), stamen___ (anther___, filament___), petal___ and sepal___

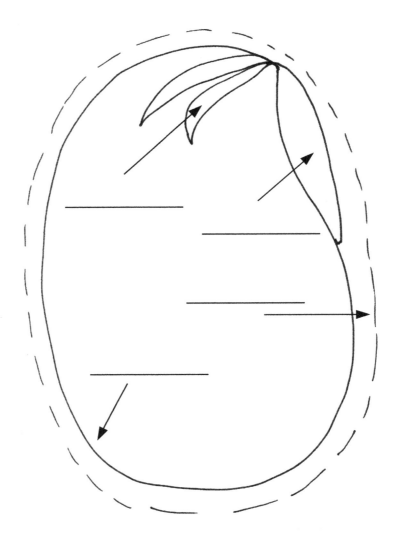

Figure B.19: Parts of a Seed

Locate and label: radicle (root), plumule (new shoot), testa (outer seed coat), and food store

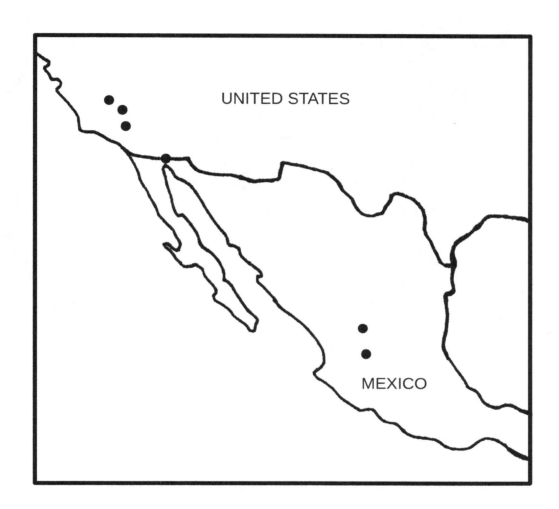

Figure B.20: Esperanza's Journey Map

Figure B.21: Butterfly Template

Appendix C

Answer Keys for Multi-Unit Activities

Answer keys for single-unit activities are found within the curriculum.

C.1   California Map Key

Figure C.1: California Map Key

C.2 Habitat Tracker A Key

Habitat	Trees/Shrubs	Flowering Plants	Animals	Location (cities)
Coast & Islands	Surf grass, eel grass, giant kelp beds (Santa Rosa Island), Channel Island trees (3 types)	Beach primrose, beach morning glory, sea palm, angelica	Western gulls, humpback whales, California sea lion, sea anemonies, acorn barnacles	San Diego, Monterey, Ventura, Santa Barbara, Mendocino, Long Beach, Carlsbad
Chaparral & Coastal Scrub	No trees, but shrubs such as toyon, scrub oak, ceanothus sagebrush, buckwheat	Mariposa lilies, fire poppies monkeyflowers	Brush rabbit, coast horned lizard, hawks, kangaroo rats	Monterey, Palos Verdes, San Diego, Santa Monica, Morro Bay
Oak Woodlands	20 species of oaks, digger pines, low shrubs like poison oak, California walnut	Flowering shrubs such as buckeye and squaw bush	Acorn woodpeckers, scrub jays, gray squirrel, mule deer	San Luis Obispo, Paso Robles, Coloma, Mariposa
Sierra Nevada	Giant Sequoia, Sierra juniper, Jeffrey pine, Douglas fir	Snow plant, lupine, red heather, paintbrush	Bighorn sheep, hermit warblers, Douglas squirrel	Kirkwood, Yosemite Valley, Grant Grove

Table C.1: Habitat Tracker, A Key

C.3 Habitat Tracker B Key

Habitat	Trees/Shrubs	Flowering Plants	Animals	Location (cities)
Coniferous Forest	Giant Sequoia, redwoods, Jeffrey pine, Ponderosa pine	Ferns, club mosses, and lichens	Banana slugs, California newt, northern spotted owl	Mendocino, Carmel, Monterey, Lake Shasta, Yosemite
Salt Marsh	Eelgrass, pickleweed, cordgrass	cattails	Avocets, bay ghost shrimp, harvest mice, ospreys, egrets	San Francisco, Arcata, Baywood/Los Osos
Desert	Big sagebrush, Joshua tree, smoke tree, creosote bush, blue palo verde	Most bushes flower: Mojave yucca, creosote bush, blue palo verde	Desert tortoise, Mojave ground squirrel, desert bighorn, coyote	Needles, Barstow, El Centro, Ridgecrest, Alturas
Grasslands	Red brome, wild oats, filarees, goldfields	California poppies, lupines, coreopsis, owl's clover	California quail, blacktailed jackrabbit, tule elk	Bakersfield, Sacramento, Fresno, Merced

Table C.2: Habitat Tracker, B Key

C.4 How We Came Tracker Key

Character	Birthplace	Migrates to	Method of transportation	Time it took to migrate	Other notes
Karana	San Nicolas Island (Nicoleño tribe)	Santa Barbara Mission	Captain Nidever's boat	a few days	
Rosalia	Suisun tribal area	Mission San Rafael	Found by Padre Ygnacio	minimal	
Junípero Serra & Sacred Expedition	Majorca, Spain	San Diego and beyond	Walked from Loreto, Mexico	6 weeks from Loreto to San Diego	
Walter & Nelly Johnston	Missouri	Sutter's Fort area	Covered wagon	6-12 months	
Jack & Praiseworthy	Boston, Massachusetts	San Francisco	*Lady Wilma* ship	5 months	15,000 miles
Cut-Eye Higgins	East Coast US	San Francisco	*Lady Wilma*	2-3 months	via mule over Panama
Chin & Ah Sing	China	Chinatown, SF	Boat	8 weeks (research)	In US for 2 years
Esperanza	Aguascalientes, Mexico	Arvin, CA	Wagon, train, truck	Several weeks	

Table C.3: How We Came Tracker Key

C.5   Map of Americas Key

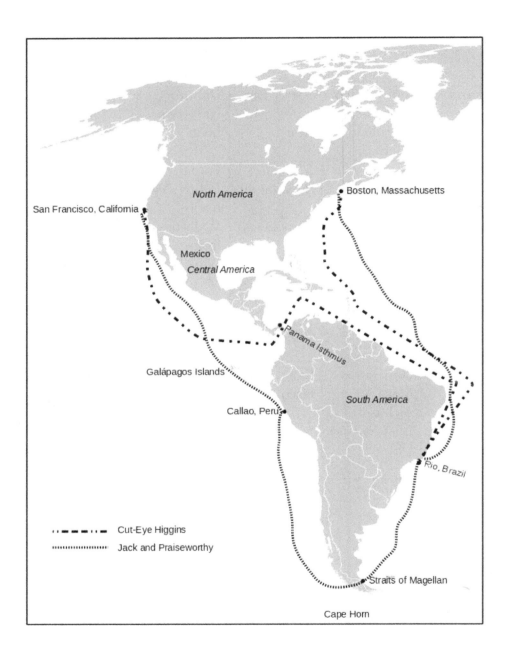

Figure C.2: Map of the Americas Key

C.6 Timeline Key

Date	Event	Page number
4.6 billion years ago	Earth's formation	49
1.7 million to 10,000 years ago	Pleistocene epoch	43
10,800BC (12,800 years ago)	Approximate year Santa Rosa pygmy mammoth died	39
1769-1782	Junípero Serra & Sacred Expedition	56
1769	First mission built (San Diego)	56
1821	Date Spain accepts Mexican independence	63
1823	Last mission built (San Francisco)	56
1834	Missions close (secularization)	63
1835	Year the Nicoleño Indians left San Nicolas Island	34
April 23, 1838	John Muir born	119
June 14, 1846	Bear Flag Revolt	79
1848	Year Mexico lost California	79
January 24, 1848	Gold discovered on American River	117
1850	California becomes a state	79
1853	Year "Karana" was rescued	32
1860-61	Pony Express	131
May 10, 1869	Golden Spike completes the Transcontinental Railroad	131
1894-1898	Dates of Pigeon Express	42
April 18, 1906	San Francisco earthquake	159
1920s	Hetch Hetchy water project completed	183
1920-30s	Jazz scene in LA on Central Ave	196
1929	Deportation Act	228
1930s	Dust Bowl	228
1994	Pygmy mammoth skeleton discovered	39
Varies	Date of family memory	38

Table C.4: Timeline Key

Appendix D

Acknowledgements

For
My two angels who smile down on me:
My beautiful Grandma Weissberg
And my mother, Kathy Wilkie

I wish to thank, profusely, my dear, dear friends and people who have encouraged me along the way. At the very top, I am grateful to my husband, Mark. He has helped me to stay with the project, generously availed himself for technical support issues regarding Latex, and offered valuable guidance about how a new writer can launch a project such as this. I also want to thank my friend Kristina Rokey, for being a springboard in getting this project from an idea to something a teacher can use (a ton) more easily. Thanks also to my librarian friend Dan McLaughlin, for reading a manuscript and encouraging me to include more on teaching research, which helps to ground the story. My father-in-law Mark Echeverri encouraged me to look at the vital issue of water, and to pause and reflect on changes in California from 1847-1850.

A big hug also goes out to Carmela Gomes; after reading my project, she encouraged me to appeal to kids' natural desire to explain the world by including both an early inventory of a student's family system and the big questions that are sprinkled throughout. Also, she likes to keep learning experiences real: her project ideas of the "towel" plate tectonics model and the back-of-the-door California Map indeed make history larger than life. I have so much more to learn from this amazing woman.

Additionally, thanks to my wonderful friend and copy editor, Kristie Savage, who took on my project under a tight deadline, and brought all of her faculties as an editor, teacher, homeschooling mom, and cheerleader to my book. I am so grateful for her expertise.

I am privileged to have my talented daughter, Camille Echeverri, participate in my project by designing a fresh, engaging cover, as well as the Appendix butterfly template. Also, thanks to the ever-talented Esther Park for the beautiful logo.

This work would be more difficult still without the generous organizations that have responded with generous permissions along the way: Kath Murdoch in New Zealand and Brandon Rumsey at David Rumsey Map Collections.

Also, thanks to my friends in education who have listened and supported me along the way – Karen Cabot, Beth Jones, Jill Frazee, Jennifer Mitchell, and Lynn and Daryl Haselton. And thanks to my sister Lisa Ellis for fact checking my botanical science and to my neighbor Alicia for reading the section on "Exploration." Finally, appreciations to my mentor: Alice Zulli, she helped me to see magic (that had secretly been there all along) and do something about it!

Also from Carrier Shell Curriculum

Earth Party! An Early Introduction to the
Linnaean System of Classification of Living Things
Unit Study
by Christine Echeverri

carriershellcurriculum.com
Curriculum — Classes — Bookstore

Made in the USA
Las Vegas, NV
14 November 2023

80866642R00188